SpringerBriefs i

We are delighted to announce SpringerBriefs in Education, an innovative product type that combines elements of both journals and books. Briefs present concise summaries of cutting-edge research and practical applications in education. Featuring compact volumes of 50 to 125 pages, the SpringerBriefs in Education allow authors to present their ideas and readers to absorb them with a minimal time investment. Briefs are published as part of Springer's eBook Collection. In addition, Briefs are available for individual print and electronic purchase.

SpringerBriefs in Education cover a broad range of educational fields such as: Science Education, Higher Education, Educational Psychology, Assessment & Evaluation, Language Education, Mathematics Education, Educational Technology, Medical Education and Educational Policy.

SpringerBriefs typically offer an outlet for:

- An introduction to a (sub)field in education summarizing and giving an overview of theories, issues, core concepts and/or key literature in a particular field
- A timely report of state-of-the art analytical techniques and instruments in the field of educational research
- A presentation of core educational concepts
- An overview of a testing and evaluation method
- A snapshot of a hot or emerging topic or policy change
- An in-depth case study
- A literature review
- A report/review study of a survey
- An elaborated thesis

Both solicited and unsolicited manuscripts are considered for publication in the SpringerBriefs in Education series. Potential authors are warmly invited to complete and submit the Briefs Author Proposal form. All projects will be submitted to editorial review by editorial advisors.

SpringerBriefs are characterized by expedited production schedules with the aim for publication 8 to 12 weeks after acceptance and fast, global electronic dissemination through our online platform SpringerLink. The standard concise author contracts guarantee that:

- an individual ISBN is assigned to each manuscript
- each manuscript is copyrighted in the name of the author
- the author retains the right to post the pre-publication version on his/her website or that of his/her institution

More information about this series at http://www.springer.com/series/8914

José Ernesto Rangel Delgado ·
Antonina Ivanova Boncheva
Editors

Knowledge Society and Education in the Asia-Pacific

Recent Trends and Future Challenges

Springer

Editors
José Ernesto Rangel Delgado
Pacific Circle Consortium &
University of Colima
Villa de Álvarez, Mexico

Antonina Ivanova Boncheva
Pacific Circle Consortium & Autonomous
University of South Baja California
La Paz, Mexico

ISSN 2211-1921 ISSN 2211-193X (electronic)
SpringerBriefs in Education
ISBN 978-981-16-2332-5 ISBN 978-981-16-2333-2 (eBook)
https://doi.org/10.1007/978-981-16-2333-2

© The Editor(s) (if applicable) and The Author(s), under exclusive license to Springer Nature Singapore Pte Ltd. 2021
This work is subject to copyright. All rights are solely and exclusively licensed by the Publisher, whether the whole or part of the material is concerned, specifically the rights of translation, reprinting, reuse of illustrations, recitation, broadcasting, reproduction on microfilms or in any other physical way, and transmission or information storage and retrieval, electronic adaptation, computer software, or by similar or dissimilar methodology now known or hereafter developed.
The use of general descriptive names, registered names, trademarks, service marks, etc. in this publication does not imply, even in the absence of a specific statement, that such names are exempt from the relevant protective laws and regulations and therefore free for general use.
The publisher, the authors and the editors are safe to assume that the advice and information in this book are believed to be true and accurate at the date of publication. Neither the publisher nor the authors or the editors give a warranty, expressed or implied, with respect to the material contained herein or for any errors or omissions that may have been made. The publisher remains neutral with regard to jurisdictional claims in published maps and institutional affiliations.

This Springer imprint is published by the registered company Springer Nature Singapore Pte Ltd.
The registered company address is: 152 Beach Road, #21-01/04 Gateway East, Singapore 189721, Singapore

Presentation

It is with great pleasure and joy that I write this presentation on behalf of the Pacific Circle Consortium. The book, *Knowledge Society and Education in the Asia-Pacific: Recent Trends and Future Challenges*; is an excellent contribution to the knowledge of and about Asia-Pacific. The research covers various Knowledge-based areas such as: "A Call to Examine Civic Discourse and Engagement in the Asia-Pacific in an Online World"; "Business and Training in a Knowledge-Based Economy Environment, The Telmex Case"; "The Knowledge Society of Russia"; "China: Compatible Relations Between the Development of Artificial Intelligence, Employment and Education"; "Higher Education, Knowledge Economy and Tourist Competitiveness in the APEC Zone"; "The Knowledge-Based Economy in Asia and the Pacific: Links with the Objectives of Sustainable Development" "Environmental Education, evolution and recent trends"; and lastly "The Knowledge Society in the Circle: The New Era of Education and Research in Asia and the Pacific."

The Pacific Circle Consortium also provides research about and among the people and countries in and around the Pacific. "In 1977, the Pacific Circle Consortium was founded as part of the Organization for Economic Cooperation and Development (OECD). PCC became independent around the mid 2000s and it currently operates as an independent, incorporated, not-for-profit organization. The vision of the Pacific Circle Consortium is for educators, researchers, and policymakers to promote international and intercultural understanding and cooperation among the people and counties in and around the Pacific. The Consortium provides a conference yearly, journals at least twice a year and projects to share knowledge, practice, and ideas in order to deepen understanding of education systems and initiatives, particularly in Indigenous, Pacific and minority education."

This is particularly important at a time, in the world, where issues of race, justice, violence, inequality, and sickness abound. We must stop and recognize that if our societies are to grow, build trust, and confidence in each other, we must rectify the wrongs of the past and create a future where all are held to be valued and worthwhile.

The United States was once known as a place of leadership and a place where the disenfranchised could go and be free. Today, they have people dying because of bungling how to deal with the coronavirus pandemic. Not only that, people of color are dying at a faster rate and the leader of the US blames Asians for the cause of the pandemic. This is of course, not limited to the US, it is a part of the intrinsic racism impacting the world, some of the ism's are manifested in macro-ism's such as the murder of Mr. Floyd in Minneapolis, Minnesota or in micro-ism's, such as not allowing indigenous people cultures not taught in school systems. There are freedoms taken away from our brothers and sisters in various places in Asia, Africa, South America, and Mexico, etc. Violence is escalating worldwide and yet people seem powerless to do anything about it.

If the global societies are to come to a "new normal" then we must create a new way of thinking, doing, and being. It is the contributions, such as those in this scholarly work, which explain what has happened and what the future can and should be. PCC chose to collaborate on this project because it is committed to providing opportunities for individuals and institutions to research and present information about Asia-Pacific people and the impact they have on the global society. Leticia Reyes Morin, in her chapter on "Business and Training in a Knowledge-Based Economy Environment: The Telmex Case," points out that:

> In other words, models where the common denominator is flexibility and open access to the population, with a new educational philosophy in the form of management and administration scholarships consequently also changes in the role of students and teachers, renewal of curricula, review of content and relevance of the same to improve skills, communication and interdisciplinary skills, entrepreneurship, in order to train them for the demand of changing labor markets, internationalization of HEIs through knowledge of the diversity of cultures, professional specialization and mastery of information and communication technologies. (Wang, 2008)

José Ernesto Rangel Delgado and Ángel Licona Michel also dealt with Knowledge Base but in the Society, opines in their chapter "The Russia's Knowledge Society."

> Although it is true that the process of human resources development (pre-school, primary and secondary education), in recent years has improved and is shaping a new generation that is preparing to be competitive both inside and outside the country. However, the skills development processes associated with new technologies seem to be distancing themselves from the main objective of the knowledge society that focuses on improving well-being as a whole. The data provided on the instruments implied by the KBS, in practice, may have perverse effects that distort their successful operation.

Aníbal Carlos Zottele Allende, Claudia Elilú Méndez Viveros and Esteban Zottele de Vega "China: Compatible Relations between the Development of Artificial Intelligence, Employment and Education," again deals with knowledge but adds to it Artificial Intelligence (AI). They define AI as:

> the capacity of a system to correctly interpret external data, to learn from this information and use it to achieve specific tasks and goals through flexible adaptation" (Kaplan & Haenlein, 2016). This type of intelligence has become relevant in recent years due to advances in science and technology (S&T) that are incorporated at high speed and that have a significant impact on world society.

The authors focus is on "the effect that the expansion of AI has had on the education sector of the PRC, favoring the creation of higher-level study plans and programs that train AI professionals, especially derived from the investment that China performs in R&D, particularly in the field of ICTs." Finally, they conclude that:

After a millennial history in which China was a central country in manufacturing and trade, it became a peripheral nation with a minimal economic impact at the global level, from the predominance of the economies of Western Europe and the United States in the late 19th century and much of the 20th century. However, it has once again become one of the leading nations of the 21st century.

Carlos Mario Amaya Molinar, Juan Carlos Yáñez Velazco, Irma Magaña Carrillo in their chapter "Higher Education, Knowledge Economy and Tourism Competitiveness in the APEC Area," take yet a different approach to knowledge economy with a focus on Tourism. They conclude that of the top 10 countries with high tourism and ability to make money are in the Asia-Pacific. They also conclude that:

> those countries that invest the most in higher education, research and development, human capital and in the factors that make up the knowledge economy are more competitive in terms of international tourism and in terms of performance in earning income per visitor. Somehow, saying this may seem self-evident, extremely obvious, but it does not seem to be so for the leaders of many countries.

José Ernesto Rangel Delgado and Antonina Ivanova Boncheva in their chapter, "The Knowledge Society in the Circle: The New Era of Education and Research in Asia and the Pacific" stated since it is not possible to explain the KBS without its close link with education. The aim of this book was to explore the knowledge-based economy and where PCC plays a fundamental role for its development and application.

> In the opinion of the authors and according to Douglas (2020), the education and the research face great challenges related to the new knowledge-based society imposed by the pandemic. Some important future aspects are the use of online learning, the strengthening of work at home, schools that are more autonomous, the increased use of ICTs, the philanthropic financing of education, the strengthening of the private school, fostering of educational models based on competences. It is very important also, the consciousness of the agents involved in education as students, parents and teachers, a consolidation of the competency-based approach, the public-private partnership as well an *ad hoc* educational policy. All these elements seem to shape the new tendencies to constitute a new KBS because of the impacts of COVID-19.

So, what does the future hold for the global societies? The first chapter by Thanh Trúc T. Nguyễn and Lauren K. Mark and last two chapters by Antonina Ivanova Boncheva and Dennis Nohemí De La Toba in the book, look at what could and is happening that offer future opportunities for Asia-Pacific and other places around the globe.

> We posit that discussions and investigation of the perceptions and experiences of upper elementary, middle, and high school students, in addition to their parents and teachers on what it means to be a digital citizen—an active, participating member of an online community is a critical need across the Asia-Pacific region… We believe research on how the Internet has influenced and changed interactions in communities in which we physically live and the communities and in which we might interact is important. Concerns have been voiced over how the Internet may be leading towards the decline of community (Bearden, 2016; Wellman & Gulia, 1999), and we believe exploration of this area and investigation of perceptions on how a person's quality of life and social well-being have been affected are vital.

The importance of being knowledgebase is very important to effectively using the internet and becoming a digital citizen.

Internet safety and digital citizenship education require a shared responsibility between parents and educators and gathering the perspectives from these three groups could help to bridge certain gaps between the home and school in these regards.

The authors conclude that a future endeavor would be to:

… encourage scholars to examination the influence of the Internet on the values of citizenship in Asia-Pacific regions to consider how digital technology has redefined citizenship and civic contributions; compare the newly defined face-to-face and online personas; reflect on how adults can provide ethical guidance, and values of citizenship and engagement in young children online; and probe the aspects of the Internet that are perceived to affect a person's social capital in terms of a sense of community.

Antonina Ivanova Boncheva, in her chapter, "The Knowledge Based Economy in Asia and the Pacific: Links to the Sustainable Development Goals" basically that "The Knowledge-Based Economy (KBE) is expanding rapidly based on innovation and technological change and human resource development. The success of the Asia and the Pacific Rim countries in the world economy is based on their capacity to implement the KBE." The author concludes that:

[1.] The ability to innovate and create knowledge—and to find innovative applications of the same—is strongly influenced by the capacity of higher education institutions. However, traditional models of higher education in Asia and the Pacific lack this capacity, which is problematic in a dynamic region with a rapidly increasing number of middle-income countries. [2.] As an issue for academic inquiry, the knowledge society has triggered ample interest across many fields, wherein there is a fierce debate between its admirers and critics. Some consider it as an historical discontinuity and other believe it represents a transformative change in the organization of society. Actually, in the days of COVID 19, we are witnessing the knowledge-based economy expanding rapidly, with all the prospects of maintaining the spaces gained in the future conditions of the new normality.

Dennis Nohemí De La Toba chapter entitled, "Some Reflections on the Evolution and the Roll of the Environmental Education," states that:

Environmental problems are the most difficult challenge facing humanity in the 21st century. They are primarily caused by the technology that prioritizes the use of natural assets for accumulation of capital concentrated in few hands.

The author concludes with eighteen reflections that need to be considered if globally we are to with the environment in ways that will not mean the destruction of the world. Again, these are issues that people of the world must deal with in the future.

In conclusion, PCC is very proud to be a partner is this book. It should be read by all because it enlightens the reader about the contributions that Asian-Pacific's have made to the global societies and it gives some direction of what to do in the future to bring humankind together based on knowledge and skills.

Dr. Rosilyn M. Carroll
Chair of PCC
Minneapolis, MN, USA
Summer of 2020

References

Bearden, S. M. (2016). *Digital Citizenship: A Community-Based Approach.* Corwin Press.

Douglas, H. N. (2020). *How Will COVID 19 Change Our Schools in the Long Run?* Brown Center Chalkboard, The Brookings Institution USA. https://www.brookings.edu/blog/brown-center-chalkboard/2020/04/24/how-will-covid-19-change-our-schools-in-the-long-run/?utm_campaign=Brookings.

Kaplan, A., & Haenlein, M. (2016). Higher Education and the Digital Revolution: About MOOCs, SPOCs, Social Media, and the Cookie Monster. *Business Horizons* (pp. 441–450). Elsevier.

Wang, Y. (2008). *Educación Superior para el Desarrollo Humano y Social en Asia y el Pacífico. Nuevos desafíos y roles cambiantes.* Universitat Politecnica de Cataluya Barcelona Tech. https://upcommons.upc.edu/handle/2099/7935.

Wellman, B., & Gulia, M. (1999). Net-Surfers Don't Ride Alone: Virtual Communities as Communities. In B. Wellman (Ed.), *Networks in The Global Village Life In Contemporary Communities* (pp. 331–366). https://doi.org/10.4324/9780429498718-11a.

Introduction

In 2019, a group of researchers published the book *Science, Technology and Innovation for Development. Experiences from the Asia-Pacific Region and Mexico,"* sponsored by the Pacific Circle of Consortium, the Autonomous University of Baja California Sur, the National Council of Science and Technology, the Center for Biological Research of the North-West, AC, the Mexican Consortium of APEC Study Centers, and the University of Colima. It was an important collaboration experience and a great success. The book is digital and is available in Spanish.

When exploring the possibility of incorporating the Pacific Circle Consortium (PCC) into this initiative, the Consortium expressed a great interest to be part of the project. As a result, the coordinators of the book committed to organize a second volume of the book, exclusively for the PCC, edited in English. We launch this book now with contributions of some members of the Consortium. It is a great honor for us to have the book presented by Dr. Rosilyn M. Carroll, Chair of the PCC.

The countries and case studies explored in this book correspond to the contributions of the authors that expressed interest to be part of this project. However it is important to mention that other members of the PCC already expressed their intention to contribute to a next stage of this study, analyzing the KBS in countries as South Korea, Australia, New Zealand, and Thailand.

To continue with the topic of Science, Technology, and Innovation for Development, the editors dedicated this volume specifically not only to the recent trends in the Knowledge Society and Education in Asia-Pacific, but also to the future challenges involved.

In this context the book presents studies on general topics related to the knowledge society of the Pacific Circle such as: "The knowledge-based economy in Asia and the Pacific: links with the objectives of sustainable development" by Antonina Ivanova Boncheva, "A Call to Examine Civic Discourse and Engagement in the Asia-Pacific in an Online World" by Thanh Trúc T. Nguyễn & Lauren K. Mark, and "Environmental Education, evolution and recent trends" by Dennis Nohemí De La Toba. The book explores also the cases of some countries within the Pacific Rim in the chapters "The knowledge society of Russia," co-authored by José Ernesto Rangel Delgado and Ángel Licona Michel, and "China: compatible relations between the development of artificial intelligence, employment and education," by Anibal Carlos Zottele Allende,

Claudia Elilú Méndez Viveros, and Esteban Zottele de Vega. The topic is explored also on sectoral level, namely the tourism, an activity of great importance for the Asia-Pacific countries by Carlos Amaya Molinar, Juan Carlos Yáñez Velazco and Irma Magaña Carrillo in the chapter "Higher Education, Knowledge Economy and Tourist Competitiveness in the APEC Zone." Finally, Leticia Reyes Morin presents a case study of a specific business in the chapter "Business and training in a knowledge-based economy environment, the Telmex case."

By the time the proposal for this volume was made, although the environmental deterioration and stress faced by society and nature, it was not possible to glimpse that it was so soon that the profound transformations in these processes would be present in the day-to-day life of the classroom in early 2020. The pandemic of COVID-19 is already causing a global crisis that would prioritize the teaching-learning processes mediated by the information and communication technologies. This is how the nature of the knowledge society, is modified and nuanced by the fears and effects that COVID-19 has caused, forcefully presenting itself as the most appropriate strategy to continue with the noble task of teaching.

Modern society has been undergoing significant changes in various spheres of social life. The transformations have enabled scholars to apply a qualitatively different approach to determine a diversity of social phenomena and their role in the modern world.

Certainly, these changes in standards and stereotypes translate into the constant transformation of human life. The analysis suggests that its basis is associated with the accumulation of knowledge and the results of fruitful use. This is because the knowledge is a constantly moving social factor that survives certain vital tests and modifies at the time that the society develops.

According to Alfred Marshall, knowledge serves as the most powerful production engine, since "it allows us to subdue Nature and compel it to satisfy our needs." Therefore, knowledge helps to advance toward a socioeconomic development based on an enlightened human being capable of assimilating the limits according to his knowledge for respectful control of nature.

Thus, the first objective of this book is to explore the theoretical framework of the KBS framed by the borders imposed by the Pacific Ocean, particularly from the perspective of the PCC, through a paradigm shift toward satisfying the human needs that must be applied to guarantee the socioeconomic conditions that future development require.

The knowledge society involves skills and competences, as well as other inherent characteristics of individuals, making it one of the most important forms of formal education. Therefore, the concept of knowledge considers two definitions of education: as an economic contribution (training) and as a system for development, which operates based on a workforce synthesis of the set of skills, knowledge, abilities, motivations, and powers embodied in a person. A system based, therefore, on the education (in all its forms) of human beings, which requires financing and an appropriate organization for the achievement of development.

In this sense, a key strategy to determine human development has been to apply the conception of a knowledge society that combines various economic concepts such as "technological change," "research," "innovation," "productivity," and "competitiveness."

The second objective of this book is to analyze how education relates to the knowledge society in the Asia-Pacific region, considering global issues such as environmental degradation, climate change, pollution, soil erosion, growth of the population, which are a cause of concern for parents, educators, civil society, and governments of the countries around the "Pacific Circle." It is necessary to change the current transformative paradigm to one that ensures environmental sustainability, with the support of scientific education and research, as an issue that must be integrated into the curricula in schools at all educational levels. The later constitutes the third objective of this book.

Thus, the contributions of the authors in general focus on the analysis on education and capacity building as two important aspects for the KBS. These allow to understand the necessity of lifelong job training according to the scientific and technological progress that societies such as China, Mexico, Russia, the United States, and New Zealand face in the Pacific Circle. Because of that, it is crucial to incorporate scientific-technological elements in the curricula of all educational levels in order to establish an educational model based on competitions, that capitalizing previous knowledge generates new contributions.

Additionally, the KBS has to be based on education, in broader terms. In the companies, but also in the schools, public or private, supported by educational models that do not stop promoting the values that give meaning to the human beings, involving them into a competition that improves the workforce and generates better social conditions. Thus, if the science, technology, and education were not included in the curricula the development of the countries would be seriously hindered. This is confirmed by the different crises faced by the societies, but particularly by the current economic crisis, aggravated now by COVID-19.

Ironically, the final opinions of the authors' in this book are not particularly new. Since the last century, with the boom of the internet and the information and communication technologies, new forms of society have been emerging that may well focus on the essence of KBS. The relevant issue in this sense is that the current health crisis ratifies the importance of the digital society. This fact confronts us with the challenge to adequate accordingly the educational process, incorporating new technologies and restructuring the school by application of distance education, and the new forms of management.

Therefore, accelerated training is required to adapt to the new conditions of the current and future society. In this sense, the studies presented in this book demonstrate that all the economy sectors as tourism, communications, finance, business, and government must recognize the importance to education, research, and development. This will be the pathway to form a solid KBS based on the competency model in the educational process. The implementation of this educational strategy will secure employment for graduates, and greater social responsibility and environmental protection of the businesses according to the Sustainable Development Objectives. Moreover, this is the way to achieve an inclusive and sustainable development and better living conditions, both globally and in particular in Asia-Pacific region.

This book intertwines the history, the evolution, and the current performance, of important organizations in the Pacific Ocean, where the PCC stands out for its objective and constant efforts to foster education and research in the region. The activities of the PCC in the region are crucial for the development of a knowledge-based society (KBS), thus promoting a Pacific Community focused on the education of the "Circle."

Finally, it is our desire to leave evidence that collaborative initiatives, like this book, foster the sense of community among the members of the PCC and that an open space always exists for permanent analysis and reflection on the education and research issues, a topic of central interest to the Pacific Circle Consortium.

José Ernesto Rangel Delgado
Antonina Ivanova Boncheva

Contents

1 **The Knowledge Society in the Circle: The New Era of Education and Research in Asia and the Pacific** 1
José Ernesto Rangel Delgado and Antonina Ivanova Boncheva

2 **The Knowledge-Based Economy in Asia and the Pacific: Links to the Sustainable Development Goals** 9
Antonina Ivanova Boncheva

3 **A Call to Examine Civic Discourse and Engagement in the Asia-Pacific in an Online World** 25
Thanh Trúc T. Nguyễn and Lauren K. Mark

4 **Some Reflections on the Evolution and the Role of the Environmental Education** 37
Dennis Nohemí De La Toba

5 **The Russia's Knowledge Society** 51
José Ernesto Rangel Delgado and Ángel Licona Michel

6 **China: Compatible Relations Between the Development of Artificial Intelligence, Employment, and Education** 65
Aníbal Carlos Zottele Allende, Claudia Elilú Méndez Viveros, and Esteban Zottele de Vega

7 **Higher Education, Knowledge Economy, and Tourism Competitiveness in the APEC Area** 79
Carlos Mario Amaya Molinar, Juan Carlos Yáñez Velazco, and Irma Magaña Carrillo

8 **Business and Training in a Knowledge-Based Economy Environment: The Telmex Case** 103
Leticia Reyes Morin

Epilogue 117

Chapter 1
The Knowledge Society in the Circle: The New Era of Education and Research in Asia and the Pacific

José Ernesto Rangel Delgado and Antonina Ivanova Boncheva

Abstract In recent decades, Asia and the Pacific region's economic significance and political influence have grown enormously. Many researchers suggest that this development will continue in the future and that the continent will play a decisive role in shaping the twenty-first century. Thus, Asia's rise has often been seen as the beginning of an "Asian Century." And science, technology, and education are the pillars for the prominent place of the Asia-Pacific in the world economy. When we talk about KBS around the Circle, we are implicitly differentiating forms of integration that exist for understanding the various issues and problems in countries/economies located in the Pacific Ocean. The most relevant are the Pacific Basin Economic Council (PBEC), the Pacific Economic Cooperation Council (PECC), the Asia Pacific Economic Cooperation (APEC), the Association of Southeast Asian Nations (ASEAN), and especially the Pacific Circle Consortium (PCC). All of these were created for specific purposes, oriented toward an inclusive and sustainable development. The aim of this chapter is to present the framework of the cooperation and integration mechanism in the Asia-Pacific that created the enabling environment to foster the knowledge-based economy and society in the region, and where PCC plays a fundamental role for its further development. Finally, we explore some implications of COVID-19 on the KBS.

Globalization and the information and communications technology (ICT) revolution are creating increasingly atomized, but ubiquitously networked, economies and societies. Because of the behavior of information and knowledge as economic goods, and because of network externalities, dramatic changes, differentiations, and synergies are emerging in the modalities of creating value. In short, national economies are

---

J. E. Rangel Delgado (✉)
Pacific Circle Consortium & University of Colima, Villa de Álvarez, México
e-mail: erangel@ucol.mx

A. Ivanova Boncheva
Pacific Circle Consortium & Autonomous University of South Baja California, La Paz, México
e-mail: aivanova@uabcs.mx

© The Author(s), under exclusive license to Springer Nature Singapore Pte Ltd. 2021
J. E. Rangel Delgado and A. Ivanova Boncheva (eds.), *Knowledge Society and Education in the Asia-Pacific*, SpringerBriefs in Education,
https://doi.org/10.1007/978-981-16-2333-2_1

becoming more knowledge-based—economies where productivity and growth have become more dependent on knowledge.

In recent decades, Asia and the Pacific region's economic significance and political influence have grown enormously, that apply in first place, to China and India. Many researchers suggest that this development will continue in the future and that the continent will play a decisive role in shaping the twenty-first century (Elder et al., 2015). Thus, Asia's rise has often been seen as the beginning of an "Asian Century," during which the global balance of power will shift toward the Far East and the West's significance will wane.

Economic and political developments usually predominate when people speak of Asia and the Pacific region's growing significance for the rest of the world. What is frequently forgotten, however, is that as globalization progresses, the region's economic and political rise has often been accompanied by fundamental processes of social transformation (Bertelsmann, 2018). These changes have, on the one hand, given rise to substantial hopes for a better future. In many places, on the other, they have led to tension and conflict—developments that are, in turn, a threat to social cohesion and political stability. In terms of their impact, these far-reaching social shifts are just as important as the region's economic and political dynamism.

A knowledge-based society refers to the type of society that is needed to compete and succeed in the changing economic and political dynamics of the modern world. It refers to societies that are well educated, and therefore rely on the knowledge of their citizens to drive the innovation, entrepreneurship, and dynamism of that society's economy (UNESCO, 2016).

When we talk about KBS around the Circle, we are implicitly differentiating forms of integration that exist for understanding the various issues and problems in countries/economies located in the Pacific Ocean. The most relevant are PBEC, PECC, APEC, ASEAN, and especially the PCC. All of these were created for specific purposes, oriented toward an inclusive and sustainable development.

The Pacific Rim Economic Cooperation (PBEC) is a business sector cooperation agency created in 1967 by Weldon B. Gibson, with the participation of business leaders from South Korea, Mexico, Hong Kong, Malaysia, and the Philippines. The main objective of the PBEC is to foster free trade and investment through cooperation in the Pacific Rim. It is currently located in Hong Kong and its organization is informal in the sense that it does not have official representation from governments around the Pacific. The Pacific Economic Community Plan, adopted at the twelfth General Council meeting in Los Angeles in 1978, aims at an economic community to coordinate solidarity and cooperation among countries in the region at different stages of development (PBEC, n.a.).

Since 1993, PBEC has been the main nongovernmental organization involved in economic cooperation in the Pacific region, acting as an independent voice of business in the Pacific. PBEC has favored the collaboration of various industries, services, and professionals, strengthening the Pacific Basin as a world leader in growth. PBEC has been a driving force in the region advocating for environmental awareness, corporate social responsibility, and transparency through working committees, policy advocacy, and partnerships with organizations such as the Asian Development Bank

(ADB)/Organization for Economic Cooperation and Development (OECD)/Pacific Economic Cooperation Council (PECC)/and the Asia-Pacific Economic Cooperation Forum (APEC).

The Association of Southeast Asian Nations, or ASEAN, was established on August 8, 1967 in Bangkok, Thailand, with the signing of the ASEAN Declaration (Bangkok Declaration) by the Founding Fathers of ASEAN, namely Indonesia, Malaysia, the Philippines, Singapore, and Thailand. Brunei Darussalam joined on January 7, 1984, Vietnam on July 28, 1995, the Lao People's Democratic Republic and Myanmar on July 23, 1997, and Cambodia on April 30, 1999, making up what are today the ten ASEAN member states (ASEAN, n.a.).

The objectives and purposes of ASEAN are the following: (1) Accelerate economic growth, social progress, and cultural development in the region through joint efforts in the spirit of equality and association to strengthen the foundations of a prosperous and peaceful community of the Southeast Asian nations; (2) Promote regional peace and stability through permanent respect for justice and the rule of law in the relationship between the countries of the region and adherence to the principles of the United Nations Charter; (3) Foster active collaboration and mutual assistance in matters of common interest in the economic, social, cultural, technical, scientific, and administrative fields; (4) Provide mutual assistance in the form of training and research facilities in the educational, professional, technical, and administrative spheres; (5) Collaborate more effectively for better use of its agriculture and industries, expansion of its trade, including studying problems of international trade in basic products, improving its transport and communication facilities, and improving the level of life of their companies; (6) Promote Southeast Asian studies; and (7) Maintain close and beneficial cooperation with existing international and regional organizations with similar objectives and purposes, and explore all avenues for even closer cooperation between them.

In their mutual relations, the ASEAN member states apply the following fundamental principles, adopted in the 1976 Treaty of Friendship and Cooperation in Southeast Asia (TAC): (1) Mutual respect for independence, sovereignty, equality, territorial integrity, and national identity of all nations; (2) The right of each State to lead its national existence free from external interference, subversion, or coercion; (3) Non-interference in the internal affairs of others; (4) Peaceful settlement of disputes; (5) Waiver of the threat or use of force; and (6) Effective cooperation between the members.

At the ninth summit in 2003, ASEAN leaders agreed on the need to establish a Community. Thus, for the 12th ASEAN Summit in January 2007, leaders signed the Cebu Declaration on Accelerating the Establishment of an ASEAN Community by 2015. In addition, the leaders adopted the ASEAN Vision 2020 on the 30th anniversary of ASEAN, as a shared vision of the organization, looking outward, living in peace, stability and prosperity, united in partnership in dynamic development, and in a community of solidary societies.

Three pillars constitute the basis of the ASEAN community: the ASEAN political security community, the ASEAN economic community, and the ASEAN sociocultural community. Each pillar has its own operating rules and, together with the

ASEAN Integration Initiative (IAI) Strategic Framework and the IAI Phase II Work Plan (2009–2015), form the ASEAN Community Roadmap (ASEAN, n.a.).

PECC is a tripartite association of high-level agents from business and industrial sector, government, academic, and other intellectual circles. All participate according to their abilities and freely discuss current and practical policy issues in the Asia Pacific region.

Established in 1980, PECC has 27 Member Committees, including one associate member and two institutional members. Each Member Committee brings together leading thinkers and decision-makers from government and business in an informal setting to discuss and formulate ideas on the major challenges facing the Asia Pacific. It regularly develops and advocates for regional policy initiatives to assist the stable economic development of the region.

The efforts of building the regional PECC community led to the establishment of the official APEC process in 1989. Now the Council is one of the three official observers of the APEC process. PECC is oriented to propose policies, it is pragmatic and preventive. Its work program aims at better policy cooperation and coordination in areas including trade, investment, and finance (PECC, n.a.).

PECC has provided information and analytical support to APEC ministerial meetings and working groups. Furthermore, it channels and facilitates the participation of the private sector in the formal process. Its objective is to serve as a regional forum for cooperation and policy coordination to promote economic development in the Asia-Pacific region, based on the premise that it is possible to articulate the strengths of business, industry, government, and academic circles. Thus, fostering economic growth, social progress, scientific and technological development, and environmental quality in the region.

The first PECC meeting (PECC I), known as "The Pacific Community Seminar," was held in September 1980 in Canberra, Australia, at the initiative of Mr. Masayoshi Ohira and Mr. Malcolm Fraser, then Prime Ministers from Japan and Australia. Eleven economies (Australia, Canada, Indonesia, Malaysia, Japan, Korea, New Zealand, the Philippines, Singapore, Thailand, and the United States) and the Pacific Island States (Papua New Guinea, Fiji, and Tonga) attended the seminar. Each delegation was composed of a senior government official, a business leader, and an academic or professional member. Representatives from the Asian Development Bank, PBEC, and PAFTAD were also present (PECC, n.a.).

From the Canberra meeting emerged the establishment of an independent regional mechanism to advance economic cooperation and market-driven integration. A vital feature of the emerging new body was its independent and unofficial status that would allow it to address economic problems as well as its possible solutions free of formal government restrictions. Therefore, it agreed on the need for an informal process involving companies and independent research institutions together with governments.

Former Prime Minister of Australia Bob Hawke firstly publicly broached the idea of APEC during a speech in Seoul, Korea, on January 31, 1989. Ten months later, 12 Asia-Pacific economies met in Canberra, Australia, to establish APEC. The founding members were Australia; Brunei Darussalam; Canada; Indonesia; Japan;

Korea; Malaysia; New Zealand; the Philippines; Singapore; Thailand; and the United States.

China; Hong Kong, China; and Chinese Taipei joined in 1991. Mexico and Papua New Guinea followed in 1993. Chile acceded in 1994. In addition, in 1998, Peru, Russia, and Vietnam joined, taking the full membership to 21.

APEC is the premier Asia-Pacific economic forum with the primary goal to support sustainable economic growth and prosperity in the Asia-Pacific region.

APEC fosters economic integration to build a dynamic and harmonious Asia-Pacific community by championing free and open trade investment, promoting and accelerating regional economic integration, encouraging economic and technical cooperation, enhancing human security, and facilitating a favorable and sustainable business environment. The initiatives turn policy goals into concrete results and agreements into tangible benefits (APEC, n.a.).

Addressing the challenges put forth by the Leaders, the project titled "Towards Knowledge-based Economies in APEC" (KBE project) was initiated by the APEC Economic Committee in the mid-1999 (APEC, 2000). Further, as a research arm for carrying out the initiative, the KBE Task Force was formed in February 2000. The aim of the KBE project was to provide the analytical basis useful for promoting the effective use of knowledge, and the creation and dissemination of knowledge among APEC economies.

The only entity fully dedicated to the international cooperation in educational research and development in the Pacific region is the Pacific Circle Consortium. It was established in 1977 as an initiative for international cooperation between educational research and development institutions in the Pacific Region, initially derived from the countries of the Organization for Economic Cooperation and Development (OECD). Australia, Canada, Japan, New Zealand, and the United States (mainland and Hawaii) attended the first meeting. Since then, membership has expanded to other countries in this region (PCC, n.a.).

Since then the focus has shifted from collaborative production of curricular materials to broader issues of educational policy development and research, as well as the organization of annual workshops and meetings, to the holding of a single annual conference. Joint projects are discussed and reported, and a variety of documents and symposia are presented. The Consortium is now independent from the OECD.

The purpose of the Pacific Circle Consortium is to promote international and intercultural cooperation between the peoples and countries of the Pacific Ocean and its surroundings. The Consortium fulfills this purpose through international, cooperative, school-related programs and activities, educational research, curriculum development, and teacher development. The Consortium shares ideas, resources, information, materials, and personnel among the countries and institutions of the Pacific and is committed to the principles of equity (PCC, n.a.).

Each year the PCC shows its intention for cultural diversity by holding its annual conference in a different member country. Recently, conferences have been held at the CNMI (Saipan, 2016), in Japan (Hiroshima, 2017), in the United States (Minnesota, 2018) and Guam-EE, United States (Tumon, 2019). In 2020, the annual conference to be held in Brisbane, Australia, was postponed to July 2021, due to the COVID-19 pandemic.

The knowledge society has become both a label policy discourse, and an issue for academic inquiry (Grewit, 2008). As a policy discourse, the knowledge society is an imperative new stage in social development characterized by a transformation in the social sphere based on new technologies, which demands a redefinition of the contract between the state, individual, and society. All regional organizations define as priority the training of human resources for development, and the development of scientific research and technology. However, PCC is the only one fully dedicated to foster the regional collaboration in research, crucial for inclusive and sustainable development in the twenty-first century. Its link as an educational branch originally recognized by the OECD, explains it largely (OECD, 2019).

Since it is not possible to explain the KBS without its close link with education. The aim of this book was to explore the knowledge-based economy and society where PCC plays a fundamental role for its development and application.

The authors explore topics related to the knowledge society; the knowledge economy and sustainable development goals; environmental education; the presence of the Pacific Islands in education along the Pacific Ocean; the digital literacy in education; the higher education and its relation to employment; the artificial intelligence and its different impacts on employment and education; as well as the capacity building for development. The book presents some cases, as China, Russia, United States, Mexico, and some reflections from the Pacific Islands, as Hawaii.

Unfortunately, the great problem of the global contagion caused by COVID-19 reached the publication of this book. The pandemic was not foreseen, partly due to the deficiencies in the environmental education. The problems in the protection of nature in the world cause pollution, create disequilibria in the ecosystems, and affect negatively the human health, because of the current industrial development model. Thus, some changes related to the great problems in the administration of schools in the face of this pandemic and its link with KBS should be considered.

It is certainly too early to talk about the impacts and strategies that COVID-19 will entail, but a high degree of creativity is already being drawn in the decision-making that characterizes this new KBS, particularly in terms of schools.

In the opinion of the authors and according to Douglas (2020), education and research face great challenges related to the new knowledge-based society imposed by the pandemic. Some important future aspects are the use of online learning, the strengthening of work at home, schools that are more autonomous, the increased use of ICTs, the philanthropic financing of education, the strengthening of the private school, fostering of educational models based on competences. It is very important also, the consciousness of the agents involved in education as students, parents, and teachers, a consolidation of the competency-based approach, the public–private partnership as well an ad hoc educational policy. All these elements seem to shape the new tendencies to constitute a new KBS because of the impacts of COVID-19.

References

APEC. (2000). *Towards knowledge based economies in APEC* (Report by APEC Economic Committee). https://www.apec.org/Publications/2000/11/Towards-KnowledgeBased-Economies-in-APEC-2000.

APEC. (n.a.). *Mission-statement*. https://www.apec.org/About-Us/About-APEC/Mission-Statement.

ASEAN. (n.a.). *About ASEAN*. https://asean.org/asean/about-asean/.

Bertelsmann Stiftung. (2018). What holds Asian societies together? Insights from the social cohesion radar. *Verlag Bertelsmann Stiftung, Gütersloh* https://www.bertelsmann-stiftung.de/fileadmin/files/BSt/Publikationen/imported/leseprobe/1770_Leseprobe.pdf.

Douglas, H. N. (2020). *How will COVID 19 change our schools in the long run?* Brown Center Chalkboard, The Brookings Institution USA, https://www.brookings.edu/blog/brown-center-chalkboard/2020/04/24/how-will-covid-19-change-our-schools-in-the-long-run/?utm_campaign=Brookings.

Elder, M., Bengtsson, M., Akenji, L., & Olsen, S. (2015). Pathways to transformative change in the Asia Pacific Region, Asia Pacific Regional Environmental Information Network (REIN) Conference, Bangkok, Thailand. https://pdfs.semanticscholar.org/69a3/37eef18a6af1195446749969208ca5013c6a.pdf.

Grewit, B. S. (2008). *Neoliberalism and discourse: Case studies of knowledge policies in the Asia-Pacific* (Thesis), Auckland University of Technology, Australia.

OECD. (2019). *Society at a glance: Asia/Pacific 2019*. OECD Publishing. https://doi.org/10.1787/soc_aag-2019-en.

PBEC. (n.a.). *Introduction to PBEC*. https://www.pbec.org/introduction-to-pbec/.

PCC. (n.a.). *The Pacific circle consortium*. http://www.pacificcircleconsortium.org/.

PECC. (n.a.). *Introduction & history*. https://www.pecc.org/about/pecc-introduction-and-history.

UNESCO (2016). *Knowledge societies policy handbook*. United Nations Educational, Scientific and Cultural Organization. http://www.unesco.org/fileadmin/MULTIMEDIA/HQ/CI/CI/pdf/ifap/knowledge_socities_policy_handbook.

Chapter 2
The Knowledge-Based Economy in Asia and the Pacific: Links to the Sustainable Development Goals

Antonina Ivanova Boncheva

Abstract The success of the Asia and the Pacific Rim countries in the world economy is based on their capacity to implement the Knowledge-Based Economy (KBE9). The UN Sustainable Development Goals (SDGs) gave us a platform to create a universal call to action to end poverty, protect the planet and ensure that all people enjoy peace and prosperity. It provided us with more guidance and metrics to measure our progress. Some of the SDGs are directly related with the main components of the KBE. The objective of this chapter is to explore how the SDGs are related to the main components of the KBE. The study is structured as following: firstly, we present a characterization of the knowledge-based economy (KBE) and its evolution in Asia and the Pacific. Secondly, we analyze the links of the sustainable development goals (SDGs) with the most important components of the KBE. Therefore, we analyze SDG 17 and SDG 9 with relation to Science, Technology and SDG 4 regarding Education. Finally, we present some brief conclusions.

Introduction

The internationalization of production is creating new incentives and opportunities and generating new pressures for knowledge acquisition. Unlike most other economic goods, knowledge often has "public good" characteristics and increasing returns to scale. Therefore, its growing importance raises new challenges for public policy. The interaction of mutually reinforcing pressures from the internationalization of business and the drive for new knowledge makes the emerging business environment quite different from anything experienced in the past. The knowledge-based economy (KBE) is expanding rapidly based on innovation and technological change and human resource development. The success of the Asia and the Pacific Rim countries in the world economy is based on their capacity to implement the KBE. The UN Sustainable Development Goals (SDGs) gave us a platform to create a universal call to action to

---

A. Ivanova Boncheva (✉)
Pacific Circle Consortium & Autonomous University of South Baja California, La Paz, México
e-mail: aivanova@uabcs.mx

© The Author(s), under exclusive license to Springer Nature Singapore Pte Ltd. 2021
J. E. Rangel Delgado and A. Ivanova Boncheva (eds.), *Knowledge Society and Education in the Asia-Pacific*, SpringerBriefs in Education,
https://doi.org/10.1007/978-981-16-2333-2_2

end poverty, protect the planet and ensure that all people enjoy peace and prosperity. It provided us with more guidance and metrics to measure our progress. Some of the SDGs are directly related with the main components of the KBE.

The objective of this chapter is to explore how the SDGs are related to the main components of the KBE. The study is structured as following: *firstly*, we present a characterization of the knowledge-based economy (KBE) and its evolution in Asia and the Pacific. *Secondly*, we analyze the links of the sustainable development goals (SDGs) with the most important components of the KBE. Therefore, we analyze SDG 17 and SDG 9 with relation to Science, Technology and SDG 4 regarding Education. Finally, we present some brief conclusions.

Knowledge-Based Economy (KBE) and Economic Development in Asia and the Pacific

The transition to a knowledge-based economy (KBE) may turn into a structural change that differs in size and pervasiveness from the incremental changes to which all economies are constantly subject. For example, The United States already gets more than half its economic growth from industries that barely existed a decade ago. Similarly, many analysts foresee that recent dramatic changes in information and communications technologies—especially the rise of the Internet—may greatly increase international trade in services (such as banking and education) that were formerly barely traded.

Addressing the challenges put forth by the Leaders, the project titled "Towards Knowledge-based Economies in APEC (KBE project)" was initiated by the APEC Economic Committee in the mid-1999 (APEC, 2000). Further, as a research arm for carrying out the initiative, the KBE Task Force was formed in February 2000. The aim of the KBE project was to provide the analytical basis useful for promoting the effective use of knowledge, and the creation and dissemination of knowledge among APEC economies.

Empirical evidence suggests that among the more advanced economies of the world, economic growth is most sustainable for those that are strong in all of the following four dimensions:

- Innovation and technological change are pervasive and are supported by an effective national innovation system (that is, a network of institutions in the public and private sector whose activities and interactions initiate, import, modify, and diffuse new technologies and practices) (ADB, 2014).
- Human resource development is universal: education and training are of a high standard, widespread, and continue throughout a person's working life (and even beyond).
- An efficient infrastructure operates, particularly in information and communications technology (ICT), which allows citizens and businesses readily and

affordably access pertinent information from around the world.

- The business environment (that is, the economic and legal policies of government, and the mix of enterprises operating in the economy) is supportive of enterprise and innovation.

Importantly, these four dimensions are precisely those that characterize a knowledge-based economy. In short, it is becoming ever more the case that the most successful economies are those that are closest to being KBEs. The strong performance of the "Asian tiger economies" over the last few decades has likewise ridden on strengths in all four of these dimensions, whereas those APEC economies, which are still at a lower level of economic development, have been weaker in at least one of these dimensions.

Basic education is a long-term investment, without which a KBE is unsustainable. In a fully developed KBE, high-quality education services that are both widely available and widely used are a major priority for the economy and society. Without this background, it is virtually impossible to build the other elements of the national knowledge base (such as Research & Development-R&D-) to the level needed by a KBE. A major responsibility of the government is therefore to ensure that such education services are in place. Secondary enrolment in both the Asian Fast-Growing Economies and the Latin American Economies falls well short of this precondition for a KBE, though some of those economies are making serious efforts to improve this.

Information and Communication Technologies (ICT) can be seen as an enabling technology for a KBE. Advanced information systems bring down the cost of information, facilitate access to wider pools of information, and promote the spread of ideas. Accordingly, a fully developed KBE has an advanced communications network and a policy and regulatory framework that encourages competition and supports the development and use of information hardware and applications. Because of the centrality of digitized information in a KBE, the telecommunications infrastructure in a KBE needs to include high bandwidth communication (which allow for the possibility of online video, and health and education services). The Most Developed Economies and the High Performing Asian Economies have the requisite policy framework in place, but continuous substantial investment is needed to bring these goals to fruition (for example, Internet penetration is still below 50% in all the case study economies). A few other APEC economies have appropriate policies in place but have a long way to go in implementing them (Elder et al., 2015).

Grewit (2008) argues that there are three ways in which emerging economies of Asia and the Pacific can pursue knowledge-based economic development in the current times: the first is learning from the KBE journey of advanced economies and making appropriate investments and policy reforms; the second is exploiting the unique strengths and endowments of the region by pursuing strategies that amplify such strengths; and the third is leveraging game-changing trends in technology and business processes that can enable emerging economies to leapfrog technology development cycles and catch up with the latest.

The result has been that states in the region show a great diversity of strategies along the state development. While some have sought to selectively conform and/or adapt to the global neoliberal regime, others have tried to counter it with instrumental visions of their own. Some countries, such as Malaysia, have devised their knowledge society vision as a counter to what they see as a cultural and economic hegemony of the West (Lu et al., 2008).

In contrast, New Zealand and South Korea's visions of knowledge society show a high degree of agreement and/or adaptability to the neoliberal strategy. Still others, such as India, have developed knowledge society visions, because of opportunities created by impacts of neoliberalism. Neoliberal pressures in shape of IMF and World Bank conditions of liberalization of economy, combined with a trend toward outsourcing of IT services from the West formed the background to the development of knowledge society vision in India. States such as India are not immune to such pressures as reflected in the attempts to justify or "sell" such policies to the masses, as the best and the only route to socioeconomic development (Grewit, 2008).

Further, adopting the knowledge society policies is proposed as the sole guarantee toward building knowledge societies. The aspects of globalization that the discourse of global institutions highlights include elimination of trade barriers; development of technology based on knowledge transfer; improved communications and transportation; standardizing products and services; and economic competitiveness, among others.

Without this background, it is virtually impossible to build the other elements of the national knowledge base, such as R&D to the level needed by a KBE. A major responsibility of governments is therefore to ensure that such education services are in place. Secondary enrolment in both the Asian Fast-Growing Economies and the Latin American Economies falls well short of this precondition for a KBE, though some of those economies are making serious efforts to improve this.

Some distinct features of the KBE and innovation in the Asian Pacific region were identified. First, national and local governments in Asia played a more significant and direct role than their counterparts in Western countries in promoting knowledge transfer and innovation through government corporation collaboration. Sarvi and Pillay (2015) documented cases that illustrate how governments provided fundamental services to corporate innovation and promoted the collaboration between national and corporate innovation systems.

Second, national culture and administrative heritage embedded in Asia Pacific histories have significant implications for knowledge transfer and innovation. Relative to Western European and North American countries, Japan was a latecomer in industrialization, which started after the 1960s. Flynn (1992), through a comparison of innovations between the United States and Japan, noted that owing to the uniqueness of Japanese culture and management styles, which emphasized consensus building, Japanese companies were more successful in the modification, improvement, and application of technologies but were "not as successful in the invention or discovery of revolutionary new technologies" (Flynn, 1992, p. 159). Similarly, Carney (2008) noted that Asian family business groups were in favor of acquiring mature technologies due to institutional and organizational constraints, such as a simple structure with little task complexity, a strategic focus on cost-price competition, as well as the disadvantageous position of being latecomers. Thus, although Asian entrepreneurs made efforts to cultivate close interpersonal relations and social networks, innovation activities in family business groups seemed to concentrate on imitation rather than development of original proprietary technologies (Carney, 2008).

Third, knowledge transfer to Asian employees encountered resistance arising from some superstitious attitudes imprinted in local cultures (Ahlstrom & Nair, 2000). This implies that knowledge transfer and development was not context free but was affected by employees' taken-for-granted values (Lu et al., 2008). To overcome this barrier in people's perception and cognition, Ahlstrom and Nair (2000) suggested that educating employees on know-why would be as important as teaching them know-how.

In knowledge policy, this manifests as (1) utilization of knowledge for enabling freedom of the market forces, and (2) promotion of market forces in knowledge enhancing activities. The first emphasis leads to the creation of knowledge legitimizing liberalization, deregulation, and privatization in social and economic policy spheres. The second emphasis leads to the commercialization of knowledge and knowledge creating institutions such as universities. These two emphases can be called knowledge in politics and the politics of knowledge respectively (Grewit, 2008).

Parallel to the political, social, and economic diversity in the Asia-Pacific region, there exists a discursive diversity in knowledge policy discourses. Within this reality, there is a twin paradox: (1) that while there is discursive diversity, national-level discourses operate within parameters set by globally dominant discourses, ideologies, institutions, and actors, and; (2) the influence of global neoliberalism at state level is constrained by local political-economic contexts and it has to contend with the historical baggage of social welfare; state-owned ICT, education, and health infrastructure; employee unionism; affirmative action, and so on. With regard to the first paradox, the globally dominant discourse is informed by the ideology of liberal capitalism that in recent times has been called neoliberalism. Global neoliberalism determines social and political regulation in nation states. Intra-state policies and institutions impacted by neoliberalism include a wide variety—social policy; trade policy; governance mechanisms; regulation of finance, and telecommunications; industry, science and technology, and innovation system; education and health system; employment relations; political participation.

SDGs and Knowledge-Based Economy

In this part, after presenting the pathway followed to adopt the SDG, we explore the links between KBE and SDG.

- Since the Rio Conference in 1992, the world has tried to advance toward the sustainable development, promoting important actions both globally and at the national level. With the Millennium Declaration in 2000, the United Nations launched a development agenda structured around the Millennium Development Goals (MDGs). Although progress has been made in achieving these goals, environmental, economic, and social conditions still leave much to be desired in large parts of the world. In recent years, considerations about the general sustainability of present and future development pathways have increased.
- With the Rio+20 Conference in 2012 and the resulting document "The future we want" the process toward the construction of a solid post-2015 development agenda began. As a result of this process, in September 2015, the 2030 agenda with 17 objectives and 169 goals was adopted by the UN, to guide the decisions that will be made over the next 15 years. The document was accompanied by a Declaration on Means of Implementation and Global Association, as well as on its follow-up and review (Boncheva & Martinez de la Torre, 2019).
- The conclusions of the Addis Ababa Conference on "Financing for Development" are an integral part of the 2030 Agenda (ADB, 2016).

To be implemented, the Agenda requires a fundamental change in the prevailing political and cultural approaches (UN, 2015). In particular:

- The Agenda marks a change in the way in which the national States see themselves and where they want to go. The quest for "economic growth at all costs," that is, the idea that increasing monetary income can solve all social problems, without considering the consequences for the environment and without addressing social inequalities, has come to an end (Lane, 2019). In addition, a much more holistic approach to development has been adopted, where social and environmental outcomes are equally valued.
- The new framework (including the principle "no one will be left behind") finally makes it clear that: Development means much more than economic growth measured in terms of GDP; Sustainability means much more than being compatible with the environment; Equality means much more than just income or the distribution of wealth.
- The SDGs cover a wide range of topics, from social (health, poverty, education, migration, gender balance, etc.) to economic (production and consumption, jobs, energy, resilience, etc.), from the medium environment (climate change, water, ecosystems, etc.) to the rule of law and governance (responsible institutions, policy coordination, transparency, effectiveness, reduction of corruption and violence, etc.).
- Human rights and gender balance are also now integrated into the 2030 Agenda (Boncheva & Martínez de la Torre, 2019).

SDG 17 Science, Technology and Innovation (STI): Key Instruments to Take World Development Toward KBE

Science, technology and innovation (STI) are a fundamental instrument to implement this new Agenda, because they allow improving efficiency in the environmental and economic spheres, developing new sustainable options to meet human needs and empower people to actively build their future (Boncheva et al., 2019).

In the SDGs, STI has an important place in Goal 17, but also as a necessary cross-cutting component to achieve several of the MDGs. Fostering innovation is part of Goal 9, which encompasses resilient infrastructure as well as inclusive and sustainable industrialization. It elevates the role of research and development policies beyond STI, characterizing them as an important means of implementation. Following the same trend, the Addis Ababa Action Agenda (AAAA) has identified some specific STI policies as the key to achieving the MDGs.

Likewise, the Paris Agreement on Climate Action includes STI issues such as promoting development and technology transfer.

Science, technology and innovation (STI), as mentioned in United Nations and OECD documents (OECD, 2015) have been recognized as one of the main drivers of productivity growth and a key lever in the long run for economic growth and prosperity. They are also vital for environmental sustainability. In the context of the new Agenda and for the achievement of the SDGs, STIs play an even more important role (SABUN, 2015). First, STIs are largely characterized by both Means of Implementation Goal 17 and an intersectoral role in achieving various Sectoral Goals. Fostering innovation is part of Sustainable Development (Millard, 2018).

SDG 9 Build Resilient Infrastructure, Promote Inclusive and Sustainable Industrialization, and Foster Innovation

Goal 9 is related to resilient infrastructure and sustainable and inclusive industrialization. In particular, Goal 9.513 determines the role of research and innovation policy also as one of the means of implementation. Furthermore, the Addis Ababa Action Agenda (AAAA), which is an integral part of the 2030 Agenda, has identified concrete policies and actions, including STI, in support of meeting the SDGs (AAAA, 2015). Finally, the negotiations at the Paris Climate COP in December 2015 addressed STI issues, highlighting cooperative action is key to facilitating and promoting technology, and proposing a framework to enhance development action and technology transfer.

In particular, the AAAA recognizes that "the creation, development and diffusion of new innovations and technologies and associated knowledge, including technology transfer on mutually agreed terms, are powerful drivers of economic growth and sustainable development." Stresses that STI strategies must be "integral elements of our national sustainable development strategies to help strengthen knowledge sharing and collaboration" and contains a full chapter on STI, underlining:

- the role of innovations, technologies, and associated know-how, including technology transfer on mutually agreed terms, as powerful drivers of economic growth and sustainable development (AAAA, 2015);
- the need to design policies that encourage the creation of new technologies, that promote research, and that support innovation in developing countries;
- the importance of an enabling environment at all levels, including enabling governance frameworks, in promoting science, innovation, technology diffusion, in particular micro-, small-, and medium-sized enterprises, as well as diversification industrial and value added to basic products;
- a commitment to promote social innovation to support social wellbeing and livelihood sustainability (UN, 2017);
- exchange of knowledge and promotion of cooperation and partnerships between stakeholders, including governments, businesses, and communities.

The Commission of Science and Technology for Development (CSTD)

For the international dimensions of the MDGs, STIs can form the basis for a new global partnership that helps foster the spirit of solidarity and cooperation. For this to happen, development cooperation must strengthen synergies with research and development entities, to generate capacities for STIs in developing countries. An important measure to move in this direction is the increase in public and private spending on research and development (including public–private partnerships).

The Commission for Science and Technology for Development (CSTD) is one of the eight functional commissions of the Economic and Social Council (ECOSOC) of the UN. Among its main functions is to advise the UN General Assembly and ECOSOC at a high level in the case of relevant science and technology issues (UN-ECOSOC, 2018). Another important function is to collaborate with the United Nations Conference on Trade and Development (UNCTAD) in the dissemination and development of research and programs on science and especially technology. UNCTAD is responsible for substantiating the CST service primarily through the creation and implementation of programs to promote international research, transfer and application of technology, especially in the least developed countries.

Collaboration between UNCTAD and CSTD is formalized by one of UNCTAD's five areas of functions called Technology, where it is mentioned that new technology policies should be identified, particularly with regard to digital applications and applications for electronic commerce. Likewise, UNCTAD declares that one of its main activities is to focus on investment, technology, and business development, boosting investments in developing countries (UNCTAD, 2018).

One of the current topics of important collaboration at present between UNCTAD and the CSTD is "The role of science, technology and innovation in ensuring food security by 2030." This program requires new and emerging technologies, including synthetic biology, artificial intelligence, and tissue engineering, to have potential implications for food security in the future of agricultural and livestock agriculture. To take advantage of such technologies, investments in research and development, human capital, infrastructure, and knowledge flows are required. Agricultural innovation and technological diffusion are also required, including a gender perspective, sustainability, and regional and international collaboration (UNCTAD, 2018).

The CSTD and UNCTAD also collaborate as observers in the Working Group on Trade and Technology Transfer (WTO, 2018), formed by the ministers of the World Trade Organization at the meeting in Doha, Qatar, in 2001. This group examines the relationship between trade and technology transfer from developed countries to developing countries, as well as ways to increase technology flows to developing countries. UNCTAD has provided valuable national case studies and is currently continuing to collaborate with the Working Group on Trade and Technology Transfer focused on further analyzing the various factors and essential agents that influence the flow of technology between countries (WTO, 2018). For its part, the WTO also follows the meetings of the CST, and the Commission on Investment, Technology and Financial Issues of UNCTAD (Islam, 2016).

Priority topics currently dealt with by the CST are the following:

1. The role of science, technology and innovation to substantially increase the share of renewable energy by 2030.
2. Develop digital skills to benefit from existing and emerging technologies, with special emphasis on the dimensions of gender and youth (CSTD, 2018).

SDG 4: Inclusive and Equitable Quality Education

SDG 4 expresses a vision to "Ensure inclusive and equitable quality education and promote lifelong learning opportunities for all" (UN, 2015). This represents a shift from the narrow focus on universal primary education in the MDG framework and goes considerably beyond the Dakar Platform of Action for Education for All (EFA), which accompanied the MDGs. The targets for SDG 4 mention expanding opportunities across all phases of education—pre-primary, primary, secondary, vocational, higher and adult education. The targets broaden the scope of education as a global project to encompass outcomes in literacy, numeracy, and wider learning including global citizenship, sustainability, and gender equality (Vladimirova & Le Blanc, 2015). Education is noted in a number of other SDG targets, e.g. SDG 3 on good health and wellbeing, SDG 5 on gender equality and women's empowerment, and SDG 8 on decent work. The SDG framework has been read as offering something for everyone working on education (UNESCO, 2016). Despite this laudably ambitious vision, there is considerable slippage in meaning between the broad values outlined in the goal statement, detailed aspiration expressed in the targets, and global indicators selected to evaluate progress (King, 2017). There are possibilities to develop a critically informed approach to metrics for SDG 4, enhancing discussion and practice to develop indicators, which more closely express the values of the goal. The possibility is considered of mobilizations for better measures (Unterhalter, 2019).

To contribute to the meaningful implementation of SDG 4.7, the UNESCO Mahatma Gandhi Institute of Education for Peace and Sustainable Development (MGIEP) conducted a study to analyze the extent to which the ideals of SDG 4.7 are embodied in policies and curricula across 22 Asian countries (Oosterhof, 2018). At one level, MGIEP aimed to establish benchmarks against which future progress can be assessed. It also argued forcefully that we must redefine the purposes of schooling to get at the fundamental challenges associated with promoting peace, sustainability, and global citizenship through education (Mochizuki, 2019). The SDG 4 comprises seven targets that deal with quality and equality for different phases of education. The first 3 targets are intended to ensure all children and adults access to quality education from early years through primary and secondary school to technical and university levels (Brissett & Mitter, 2015). Target 4.4 aims to enhance skills for youth and adults linked to work. Target 4.5 is concerned with the distribution of educational access across a range of demographics noting the needs of people with disabilities, indigenous peoples, and vulnerable groups. Target 4.6 aims to ensure literacy and numeracy for all youth and substantially reduce adult illiteracy. Target 4.7 is the only target that deals with the content of education aiming to develop knowledge and skills for sustainable development, human rights, gender equality, and cultures of peace and nonviolence.

In addition, three targets (4A, 4B, 4C) are constructed as the means of implementation of the quality and equality targets. Target 4A aims to build and upgrade education facilities that are child, disability, and gender sensitive providing safe, inclusive, and effective learning environments. Target 4B singles out enhancing access to higher education and aims to expand the number of higher education scholarships available to developing states and African countries. Target 4C is concerned to increase the supply of qualified teachers.

SDG 4 emerged from the extensive consultations between 2012 and 2015 as a victory for proponents of a vision of quality education that was free, inclusive, and orientated to equalities. Set against this was a more limited vision for the goal, put forward by some powerful voices, arguing for a focus on narrowly defined learning outcomes for youth. While proponents of the discourse of rights and inclusion prevailed with regard to the text of the goal and the targets, they had less access to the process of developing indicators, partly because of institutional histories associated with developing education metrics, and partly because the global Education for All (EFA) movement had mobilized to secure the text on the targets, but did not maintain this for the debate around indicators.

Unlike the very limited process associated with formulating the MDGs, extensive consultation was associated with framing SDG 4 (Dodds et al., 2016). Some lobby groups were linked to education sectors (basic, secondary, or higher education), some to groupings of governments (donors or regional formations), some to interest groups, such as disability, gender, or indigenous rights (Sayed & Ahmed, 2018). The loose EFA movement was a major player, linking together civil society organizations, trade unions, NGOs, academic networks, bilateral and multilateral organizations with UNESCO taking the lead, but UNICEF and the World Bank are also key figures (Tikly, 2017). From 2000 the private sector, notably multinational corporations in ICT, had become increasingly active and well-connected in the EFA movement, working partly through Foundations and partly as providers (Sayed & Ahmed, 2018).

Tikly (2017), reflects on the EFA movement and the formulation of SDG 4, depicting this as a form of global governance, in which a group of powerful actors engaged in a process of building and maintaining legitimacy. He shows how the formulation of principles, norms, rules, and decision-making procedures around EFA had the effect of generating particular discourses, which accommodated tensions and contradictions within and between economic, sociocultural, and political perspectives. Also evident are disputes regarding which principles were considered core and peripheral (Reynolds et al., 2017), whether scrutiny of processes was more or less mobilized at particular moments, and where the limits of a discourse around equity and inclusion came to be set.

As previously noticed the Rio+20 meeting mandated the formulation of the SDGs. Key consultations on education took place in the 3 years (2012–2015) before the goal and targets were finalized. The discussion on the indicators has continued for 3 years (2015–2018) after the UN General Assembly agreed the goal and targets. Unterhalter (2019) presents an abbreviated history of these discussions and identifies the moments when particular constituencies made significant inputs into framing SDG 4. In early phases proponents of more limited focus for the goal and targets made headway, but later the discourses associated with quality and equality prevailed, most significantly with regard to free education and more substantive meanings of gender equality.

The EFA consensus building process asserted itself in mobilizing against the more technocratic vision, in May 2014 a global EFA meeting was convened in Muscat, with invitations extended by the Director-General of UNESCO to Education and Finance Ministers, a large number of country delegations, officials of multilateral and bilateral organizations, senior representatives of civil society and private sector organizations. This reviewed the focus and targets for the SDGs and issued the Muscat Agreement largely in line with the UNESCO position of April (UNESCO, 2014).

In December 2014, the UN Secretary-General published a Synthesis report which endorsed the more expansive version of SDG goal 4 that had been formulated in the OWG and set out a broad vision of education supporting the dignity and prosperity of people and the protection of the planet (UN, 2014).

The World Education Forum took place in Incheon, Korea, in May 2015. Here, a wide gathering of education Ministers, civil society activists, and seven UN organizations with an interest in education adopted the Incheon Declaration Education 2030: Toward inclusive and equitable quality education for lifelong learning giving detail and depth to realizing the goal (World Education Forum, 2015).

Other important moment was the adoption of a Framework for Action for the Incheon Declaration by high-level education sector representatives from 184 countries at UNESCO headquarters on November 4, 2015. The Incheon and Paris documents align closely with SDG 4 and this ensured the EFA movement was not on a separate track to the SDGs, as had happened with the MDGs (Vladimirova & Le Blanc, 2015). Thus, consensus had been built around inclusion and equalities as key features of the goal and this was maintained with regard to the targets. However, the narrower interpretation, which focused heavily on interpreting quality as learning outcomes, continued to be actively promoted (Sayed & Ahmed, 2015). This view was less evident in the formulation of the targets, but appeared clearly in discussion of the indicators, partly because of the institutional architecture of the metrics as discussed in the following sections.

Contested Meanings of Quality and Equalities: Formulating Targets

Although the goals and targets for SDG 4 were agreed in 2015, struggles over the meanings of quality and equalities continued, partly masked by a politics of consensus building. The conflict hinged on narrow versus broad conceptions of these terms and the institutional histories of different organizations and governments, which supported different interpretations. Tikly (2017) identifies areas of tension around EFA, and these are evident in many of the discussions associated with the formulation of the SDG 4 targets at the eight moments outlined above. The contestation between the narrow and the broad approach to quality and equalities are evident in:

- Debates about education sub-sectors, and whether to make the SDG targets focus on primary and secondary school, or include early years, further, higher, adult and vocational education.
- Whether to focus on quantities of enrolment, attendance, and progression or quality variously defined.
- How to define quality education, and whether this entailed a simple focus on learning outcomes or entailed free education, inclusion and contentious areas of value, like sustainability, rights, and gender equality.
- Whether the meaning of equitable education was limited to expanding formal rights to education to excluded groups or entailed more substantial acknowledgment of intersectional inequalities entailing redress of disadvantage and transformation of injustice within and beyond education.
- The relative position of states and markets, and how to engage with the considerable growth of the private sector in education, a discussion that came to be expressed partly as a dispute around the nature of accountability.

These contestations pre-dated the SDG process (McGrath & Gu, 2015; Mundy et al., 2016), but had considerable influence on discussions of target, and are still valid today.

Conclusions

The 2030 Agenda and its SDGs represent a new long-term perspective on development that must be reflected in a broad policy framework that encompasses all dimensions of sustainable development and that must be reflected in the decision-making of governments, companies, and individuals. The knowledge economy based on science, technology, innovation, and education, are fundamental ingredients of such change, because they allow improving efficiency both in the economic and environmental sense, developing new more sustainable ways of satisfying human needs, overcoming historical divisions, as well as empowering people to manage their own future.

The global discourse on social development and economic growth in the developing world is guided by a vision about knowledge-based economies wherein knowledge workers play an increasingly important role and the centrality of "knowledge" underpins competitiveness. The ability to innovate and create knowledge—and to find innovative applications of the same—is strongly influenced by the capacity of higher education institutions. However, traditional models of higher education in Asia and the Pacific lack this capacity, which is problematic in a dynamic region with a rapidly increasing number of middle-income countries. This dynamic growth creates a strong demand for investment in strengthening innovation and development toward a knowledge-based economy. The responsibility of governments is therefore to ensure that advanced education services are in place. Secondary enrolment in both the Asian Fast-Growing Economies and the Latin American Economies falls well short of this precondition for a KBE, though some of those economies are making serious efforts to improve this.

There are three ways in which emerging economies of Asia and the Pacific can pursue knowledge-based economic development in the current times: the first is learning from the KBE journey of advanced economies and making appropriate investments and policy reforms; the second is exploiting the unique strengths and endowments of the region by pursuing strategies that amplify such strengths; and the third is leveraging game-changing trends in technology and business processes that can enable emerging economies to leapfrog technology development cycles and catch up with the latest.

The knowledge society has become both a label policy discourse, and an issue for academic inquiry. As a policy discourse, the knowledge society is an imperative new stage in social development characterized by a transformation in the social sphere based on new technologies, which demands a redefinition of the contract between the state, individual, and society. Countries that embrace this change and formulate policies to maximize its impact are in a position to integrate in a globalized world, generate dividends in the economic sphere, and ensure general progress. Like any revolution in production, the knowledge economy will bring positive and negative externalities, job losses being highly visible among the latter. The digital economy will present challenges for law, accounting, and banking.

As an issue for academic inquiry, the knowledge society has triggered ample interest across many fields, wherein there is a fierce debate between its admirers and critics. Some consider it as an historical discontinuity and others believe it represents a transformative change in the organization of society. Actually, in the days of COVID-19, we are witnessing the knowledge-based economy expanding rapidly, with all the prospects of maintaining the spaces gained in the future conditions of the new normality.

References

ADB. (2014). *Innovative Asia: Advancing the knowledge-based economy—Highlights of the forthcoming ADB study report*. https://digitalcommons.ilr.cornell.edu/intl.
ADB. (2016). *First high-level follow-up dialogue on financing for development*. https://www.unescap.org/events/apffd-rok.
Addis Ababa Action Agenda (AAAA). (2015). http://www.un.org/esa/ffd/wpcontent/uploads/2015/08/AAAA_Outcome.pdf.
Ahlstrom, D., & Nair, A. (2000). The role of know-why in knowledge development within biomedicine: Lessons for organizations. *Asia Pacific Journal of Management, 17*, 331–351. https://doi.org/10.1023/A:1015817810935.
APEC. (2000). *Towards knowledge based economies in APEC* (Report by APEC Economic Committee). https://www.apec.org/Publications/2000/11/Towards-KnowledgeBased-Economies-in-APEC-2000.
Boncheva, A., Beltrán, L.F. y J. E. Rángel Delgado (2019). Introducción. En Boncheva, A., Beltrán Morales, L.F., y Rangel Delgado, J.E. (Eds.), *Ciencia, Tecnología e Innovación para el Desarrollo. Experiencia de la región Asia-Pacífico y México* (pp. 7–13). UABCS/CIBNOR/CONACYT/Consorcio Mexicano de Centros de Estudios APEC/Pacific Circle Consortium.
Boncheva, A., y Martínez de la Torre, J. A. (2019) "El papel de la ciencia, tecnología e innovación para
alcanzar los Objetivos de Desarrollo Sustentable" en (Boncheva, A., Beltrán Morales, L.F., Rangel Delgado, J.E., ed.) Ciencia, Tecnología e Innovación para el Desarrollo. Experiencia de la región Asia-Pacífico y México, UABCS/CIBNOR/CONACYT/Consorcio Mexicano de Centros de Estudios APEC/Pacific Circle Consortium, pp. 33–58. ISBN: 978-607-7777-97-7.
Brissett, N., & Mitter, R. (2015). The many meanings of quality education: Politics of targets and indicators in SDG4. *Journal for Critical Education Policy, 15*(1), 181–204. http://www.jceps.com/archives/3326.
Carney, M. (2008). The many futures of Asian business groups. *Asia Pacific Journal of Management, 25*, 595–613. https://doi.org/10.1007/s10490-008-9092-5.
Commission on Science and Technology for Development (CSTD). (2018). *Twenty-first Session, 14–18 May 2018, Palais des Nations Geneva, Switzerland*. http://unctad.org/en/pages/MeetingDetails.aspx?meetingid=1670.
Dodds, F., Donoghue, A. D., & Roesch, J. L. (2016) *Negotiating the sustainable development goals: A transformational agenda for an insecure world*. Taylor & Francis. Education and Development and Routledge.

Elder, M., Bengtsson, M., Akenji, L., & Olsen, S. (2015). Pathways to transformative change in the Asia Pacific Region, Asia Pacific Regional Environmental Information Network (REIN) Conference, Bangkok, Thailand. https://pdfs.semanticscholar.org/69a3/37eef18a6af1195446749969208ca5013c6a.pdf.

Flynn, B. B. (1992). Managing for quality in the US and in Japan. *Inform Journal of Applied Analytics, 22*(5), 1–89. https://doi.org/10.1287/inte.22.5.69.

Grewit, B. S. (2008). *Neoliberalism and discourse: Case studies of knowledge policies in the Asia-Pacific* (Thesis), Auckland University of Technology, Australia. https://www.adb.org/sites/default/files/publication/472021/governance-brief-033-sdgs-implementation-2030-agenda.pdf.

Islam, E. (2016). *Financial inclusion in Asia and the Pacific*. Discussion Paper First High-Level Follow-up Dialogue on Financing for Development in Asia and the Pacific Incheon, Republic of Korea. https://www.unescap.org/sites/default/files/12.Financial%20inclusion_Ezasul%20Islam_0.pdf.

King, K. (2017). Lost in translation? The challenge of translating the global education goal and targets into global indicators. *Compare: A Journal of Comparative and International Education, 47*(6), 801–817.

Lane, A. (2019). Open education and the sustainable development goals: Making change happen. *Journal of Learning for Development, JL4D, 4*(3), 275–286. https://jl4d.org/index.php/ejl4d/article/view/266/255.

Lu, Y., Tsang, E. W. K., & Peng, M. W. (2008). Knowledge management and innovation strategy in the Asia Pacific: Toward an institution-based view. *Asia Pacific Journal Management, 25*, 361–374. https://doi.org/10.1007/s10490-008-9100-9.

McGrath, S., & Gu, Q. (2015). *Routledge handbook of international education and development*. Routledge. https://www.routledgehandbooks.com/doi/10.4324/9781315797007.

Millard, J. (2018). *How social innovation underpins sustainable development*. The Social Innovation Landscape–Global Trends https://www.socialinnovationatlas.net/fileadmin/PDF/einzeln/01_SI-Landscape_Global_Trends/01_07_How-SI-Underpins-Sustainable-Development_Millard.pdf.

Mochizuki, Y. (2019). Rethinking schooling for the 21st century: UNESCO-MDGIEPs contribution to SDG 4.7. Sustainability. *The Journal of Record, 12*(2), 88–92. https://doi.org/10.1089/sus2019.29160.

Mundy, K., Green, A., Lingard, B., & Verger, A. (2016). *Handbook of global education policy*. Wiley.

OECD. (2015). *Daejeon ministerial declaration on science, technology and innovation policies for the global and digital age*. OECD DSTI/STP/MIN(2015)1 http://www.oecd.org/science/sci-tech/stiministerial-2015.htm.

Oosterhof, P. D. (2018). Localizing the sustainable development goals to accelerate implementation of the 2030 agenda for sustainable development. The current state of sustainable development goal localization in Asia and the Pacific. *ADB Governance Brief*. http://www.adb.org/publications/series/governance-briefs.

Reynolds, M., Blackmore, C., Ison, R., Shah, R., & Wedlock, E. (2017). The role of systems thinking in the practice of implementing sustainable development goals. In W. Leal Filho (Ed.), *Handbook of sustainability science and research*. Springer.

Sarvi, J., & Pillay, H. (2015). *Innovations in knowledge and learning for competitive higher education in Asia and the Pacific Region*. Asian Development Bank.

Sayed, Y., & Ahmed, R. (2015). Education quality, and teaching and learning in the post-2015 education agenda. *International Journal of Educational Development, 40*, 330–338.

Sayed, Y., & Ahmed, R. (2018). The 2030 global education agenda and the SDGs: Process, policy and prospects. In A. Berger, M. Novelli & H. Altinyelkinen (Eds.), *Global education policy and international development: New agendas, issues and policies* (pp. 185–207). Bloomsbury.

Scientific Advisory Board of the UN Secretary General (SABUN). (2015). *The crucial role of science for sustainable development and the post-2015 development agenda*. http://en.unesco.org/un-sab/sites/unsab/files/Preliminary%20reflection%20by%20the%20UN%20SG%

20SAB%20on%20the%20Crucial%20Role%20of%20Science%20for%20the%20Post-2015%20Development%20Agenda%20-%20July%202014.pdf.

Tikly, L. (2017). The future of education for all as a global regime of educational governance. *Comparative Education Review, 61*(1), 1–36.

UNESCO. (2014). Education for all global monitoring report: Teaching and learning: Achieving quality for all. UNESCO Publishing.

UNESCO. (2016). *Knowledge societies policy handbook*. United Nations Educational, Scientific and Cultural Organization: Paris. Internet: http://www.unesco.org/fileadmin/MULTIMEDIA/HQ/CI/CI/pdf/ifap/knowledge_socities_policy_handbook.pdf. Last accessed 9 August 2017.

United Nations (UN). (2014). *The road to dignity by 2030. synthesis report of the secretary general on the post 2015 agenda*. United Nations.

United Nations (UN). (2015, September 25), Transforming our world: The 2030 agenda for sustainable development. Finalized text for adoption, (A/70/L.1), New York, NY [Google Scholar].

United Nations (UN). (2017). United Nations Social Development Network. *Asia-Pacific countries use social innovation to face ageing population and gender inequality*. http://unsdn.org/2017/03/20/asia-pacific-countries-use-socialinnovation-to-face-ageing-population-and-gender-inequality/.

United Nations Conference on Trade and Development (UNCTAD). (2018). *The role of science, technology and innovation in ensuring food security by 2030*. http://unctad.org/en/pages/PublicationWebflyer.aspx?publicationid=1774.

United Nations Economic and Social Council (UN-ECOSOC). (2018). *Subsidiary bodies of ECOSOC*. http://www.un.org/en/ecosoc/about/subsidiary.shtml.

Unterhalter, E. (2019). The many meanings of quality education: Politics of targets and indicators in SDG4. *Global Policy, 10*(1), 39–51. https://doi.org/10.1111/1758-5899.12591.

Vladimirova, K., & Le Blanc, D. (2015). *How well are the links between education and other sustainable development goals covered in UN flagship reports? A contribution to the study of the science-policy interface on education in the UN system*. Department of Economic & Social Affairs. DESA Working Paper (146). https://sustainabledevelopment.un.org/content/documents/2111education%20and%20sdgs.pdf.

World Education Forum. (2015). *Education 2030. Incheon declaration and framework for action*. UNESCO (in association with UNICEF, UNDP, World Bank, UNHCR, UNwomen, UNFPA).

World Trade Organization (WTO). (2018). *The future of world trade: How digital technologies are transforming global commerce* (World Trade Report 2018). https://www.wto.org/english/res_e/publications_e/world_trade_report18_e.pdf.

Chapter 3
A Call to Examine Civic Discourse and Engagement in the Asia-Pacific in an Online World

Thanh Trúc T. Nguyễn and Lauren K. Mark

Abstract The rapid pace of technology evolution, the affordability and access to more devices, and the ease at which technology users can get away with certain online behaviors have unintentionally created cyber problems that society is not prepared to face physically, socially, mentally, emotionally, and legally. In an online culture permeated with high-speed technology and a wide variety of communication mediums to choose from, the twenty-first-century digital society perhaps has required the membership of a new type of citizen. The problem is that digital citizens are socialized by peers, not by the generations before them who more or less understand rules and regulations, right from wrong, and good from bad. With a lack of foundational levels of understanding and awareness of what digital citizenship is and what it should look like in terms of appropriate and inappropriate online behavior, it creates a humanistic problem worth considering. We posit that examination of the evolution of a digital society that has emerged in the Information Age is needed to redefine the values of citizenship and community and propose four guiding questions in this pursuit. We additionally suggest that the integration of family and school groups in the efforts to understand online civic discourse and engagement is critical to benefit not only students and educators within schools, but also the parents and community members who support schools.

Introduction

Throughout history, new communication technologies, from books to telegrams to television to telephones, have provided the basis for discussions of differences among generations. The Internet is yet another technology that has come along to contribute generational difference debates. The Internet, however, is unique, as it is an instantaneous repository and disseminator of information, unlike previous technologies. No longer does the populace need to gather to hear Socrates orate. No longer does the

T. T. T. Nguyễn (✉) · L. K. Mark
University of Hawai'i at Mānoa, Honolulu, HI, USA
e-mail: nguyen@hawaii.edu

© The Author(s), under exclusive license to Springer Nature Singapore Pte Ltd. 2021
J. E. Rangel Delgado and A. Ivanova Boncheva (eds.), *Knowledge Society and Education in the Asia-Pacific*, SpringerBriefs in Education,
https://doi.org/10.1007/978-981-16-2333-2_3

printed word have limited distribution. No longer does the child wait for the parent or teacher to answer a question; children can find answers to their own inquiries quickly and easily using a cell phone or other digital device at hand. Whether the gathered information is opinion or fact is questionable, but an answer always seems to be there.

One of our most prominent, unalienable rights in the United States is the freedom of speech. We contribute freely and often to civic discourse and uphold that right keenly as U.S. citizens. However, the lack of social presence when using a digital tool and the ability to shield one's persona behind an alias has changed how people communicate with one another online. People are quicker to add their two cents in online conversations, present their biases and opinions with minimal fear of retaliation, and say negative things they would not normally say in face-to-face contexts. The lack of empathy when sitting behind a computer screen or with a small Internet-enabled mobile device disassociates people from the fact that there are real people on the other side of their two cents. With the increase in affordability and access to Internet-enabled devices come unforeseen issues of technology misuse, such as cyber victimization, online piracy, plagiarism, and other various types of health and safety issues.

Because of potential exposure to inappropriate topics, schools originally thought to limit access to the Internet. However, after a period of fear and cutoff, schools are moving toward providing more access, which equates to greater opportunities for young learners (Technology Counts, 2015; Zhao & Frank, 2003). Nadine Holdsworth (2007) argued that "young people must have access to, and creative engagement in, local spatialities if they are to develop skills of effective citizenship" (p. 237). Holdsworth referred to actual physical spaces, namely in her argument for the need for open public spaces, such as parks, playgrounds, theaters, and studios. We believe these arguments are equally valid when considering digital or virtual spaces.

As schools have provided more Internet access for students, they have also subsequently encountered issues of poor online behavior, like plagiarism, piracy, impersonation, and sexting (Liau et al., 2005). *Cyberbullying* became a big buzzword in the early 2000s, and many research studies proliferated (Nguyen & Mark, 2014). Not surprisingly, children who use the Internet to explore and express themselves are finding themselves confronted with opinions that carry both positive and negative connotations, as well as choices that carry both positive and negative consequences. An overall lack of social presence (Short et al., 1976) when using digital tools and the ability to shield one's persona behind an online alias has redefined our ideas of social discourse and interactions. People are quicker to add their opinions in online conversations with minimal fear of retaliation.

Inappropriate social commentary and sharing is not only seen in children. We see an abundance of questionable comments and acts by adults on the Internet. News stories, blogs, discussion forums, and more give the visitor a chance to like, share, pin, tweet, and be downright rude in comments (Berson et al., 2008). Website moderators continuously tread a fine line between allowing freedom of speech and removing hate speech and inappropriate online material. With freedom of speech controversies at prominent U.S. universities making news headlines (Madhani & Yu, 2015; Paul,

2015), and secret high school sexting scandals rocking an entire Colorado town (Martinez, 2015), how do we—"digital citizens"—get at the crux of the problem? The problem lies not with the proliferation of technology, but with the core values and priorities at the heart of a society.

While we believe it is critical to identify whether youth are knowledgeable of the tenets of appropriate technology use, it is also important to understand their specific roles and responsibilities, as well as those of the adults who place these tools in their hands (Mueller & Wood, 2012). Do adults need education in digital citizenship also? We posit that discussions and investigation of the perceptions and experiences of upper elementary, middle, and high school students, in addition to their parents and teachers on what it means to be a digital citizen—an active, participating member of an online community is a critical need across the Asia-Pacific region. A comparative examination between adults and children of the influence of the Internet on the values of citizenship in light of the growing influx of digital technology can be guided by asking the following questions:

- How has the permeation and rapid adoption of digital technology redefined citizenship and civic contributions in a digitally connected society?
- How is citizenship perceived and personally defined in face-to-face circles and in online circles; what are the major similarities and differences in these two arenas?
- How can adults provide ethical guidance and values of citizenship and engagement in young children if they are not completely versed in these values themselves?
- What aspects of the Internet are perceived to affect a person's social capital in terms of a sense of community?

We believe research on how the Internet has influenced and changed interactions in communities in which we physically live and the communities and in which we might interact is important. Concerns have been voiced over how the Internet may be leading toward the decline of community (Bearden, 2016; Wellman & Gulia, 1999), and we believe exploration of this area and investigation of perceptions on how a person's quality of life and social wellbeing have been affected are vital.

Digital Citizenship

The Internet has changed how we communicate and possibly how we behave and edit ourselves before offering our opinions. The rapid pace of technology evolution, the increased affordability and access to more devices, and the ease at which technology users can get away with certain online behaviors have unintentionally created cyber problems that society was not prepared to face physically, socially, mentally, emotionally, and legally (Oxley, 2010). In an online culture permeated with high-speed technology and a wide variety of communication mediums, the twenty-first-century digital society perhaps requires the membership of a new type of citizen—the digital citizen.

Ribble and Bailey (2007) defined digital citizenship as "using technology in good, appropriate ways as well as balancing it with other skills such as interpersonal relations, self-confidence, and exercise" (p. 1). But, is that what people consider when they think of digital citizenship? Recent scholars in education base their explorations on Ribble and Bailey's definition, but it is unclear if this is the best definition. Being kind, helpful, and respectful are all ideals of citizenship toward which we strive. However, how is the idea of being "good" and self-moderating our behaviors online considered part of digital citizenship? How do we move toward personally responsible, participatory, and justice-oriented citizenship in a digital world? There is no true online government; no tangible virtual environment; no defined Internet population. The sense of shared society is a virtual one, and that society morphs as the individual chooses what they want to engage in and what they want to ignore. Is citizenship even the word to use, or, is it behavior and ethics?

A Dual Life: Digital Identity

Online societies provide a unique context and venue for people to explore various personas and use images to represent themselves in ways that could vary much or little from their offline identities (Yee et al., 2007). However, online actions can often have direct and indirect offline consequences, thus blurring the lines between "real" and "virtual" identities (Zhao et al., 2008). In a study on the comparison of online and offline identities on the social networking site, Facebook, Zhao et al. (2008) found that Facebook identities tend to represent people in socially desirable ways, where people have the ability to "stretch the truth a bit" to express how they aspire to be offline, rather than how they are actually perceived by others in "real life" (p. 1819).

Stephens et al. (2007) concluded that when it comes to online behaviors, the Internet has created a perfect venue for some people to feel more comfortable copying, plagiarizing, and cheating on academic assignments, as opposed to performing these same behaviors offline. Contributing to the growing list of online behaviors that neglect real-world ethics, in a study on digital piracy, technology users were found to participate more in the stealing of digital materials when they believed they would not get caught (Al-Rafee & Cronan, 2006). Additionally, a study in the United Kingdom found that those who possess higher Internet self-efficacy (one's personal belief in their proficiency using Internet) perceive criminal behavior online differently than those with lower self-efficacy (Millman et al., 2012).

Youth are typically motivated by the social expectations of their peers, and the online world gives these youth the venue to freely experiment with different personas and mold and bend in various social directions. However, at the opposite end of the connectedness spectrum is rejection, which can sometimes have extremely harmful outcomes for those who cannot fulfill the need of belonging and acceptance.

Civic Discourse and Engagement in a Changing Environment

Santo et al. (2010) embraced the ideas of fostering civic engagement among teens through the use of technology. They found that young people have the potential to contribute tremendously to their communities and neighborhoods by using technology in positive ways (e.g., by posting community stories, photos, and blogs online). However, young people, often called Millennials (Howe & Strauss, 1991) or Digital Natives (Prensky, 2001), have also been highly scrutinized over their questionable communication skills, readiness to join the workforce after high school or college, and their participation in civic activities. Thurlow and Bell (2009) found that older generations often perceive modern-day (text) messages negatively as a jumbled hodgepodge of letters, numbers, and symbols. Yet, a closer look at these messages revealed that shorthand language in digital messages included a playfulness, wittiness, and creativity that traditional online discourse sometimes lacks. The new ways of carrying on meaningful conversations among today's Millennials are just different, and Thurlow and Bell (2009) stated that instead of fixating on the generational differences between old and young technology users, we need to recognize "young people's uses of technology as embedded cultural practices" and start adapting to changing times (p. 1044).

In regard to civic engagement, researchers have found that young people are not as interested in government politics and voting as previous generations and prefer more involvement in community service (Mossberger et al., 2007; Syvertsen et al., 2011). Rubin (2007) found that U.S. students have a wide array of experiences, understanding, and awareness when it comes to knowing their roles as American citizens and what it means to participate in civic life. These students gain much of their civic knowledge from their everyday experiences in online environments, rather than from textbooks or class lessons. Roles and responsibilities as citizens may vary so much or be unclear because many young people do not necessarily adhere to similar or traditional definitions of what it means to be a citizen (Hickey, 2002), especially in an ever-changing online world.

Possible Frameworks

Family, School, and Community Partnerships

Epstein (1987) maintained that school is an extension of the home culture, within a larger sense of community. When these groups work in unison, the home, school, and community are the three key elements that can help the academic, developmental, and social success of a student. From a behavioral perspective, in addition to academic success, parent and school partnerships have been found to improve student behavior and can help to reduce student aggression and school violence (Sheldon

& Epstein, 2002). Based on Bronfenbrenner's (1981) ecological theory, a major component to successful partnerships is the presence of a common message of core values that a child's home, school, and community share. Internet safety and digital citizenship education require a shared responsibility between parents and educators and gathering the perspectives from these three groups could help to bridge certain gaps between the home and school in these regards. Researchers have continuously emphasized the importance of cyber ethics education extending beyond the student population to the adult population of parents and educators (Baum, 2005; Nguyen, 2011; Waters et al., 2009), and they believe that school, family, and community partnerships could help in this particular endeavor.

The idea of having parents, school faculty, and the community on the same page is not a novel concept. Especially when many factors can influence the safety and climate of a school, it becomes critical for parents, educators, as well as invested community members to contribute their efforts to increase cyber and physical safety. Epstein's (2010) theory on school, family, and community partnerships shows that it is possible for members of different groups who share common interests, goals, and responsibilities for children to come together to create better opportunities for students. DuFour and Mattos (2013) and Marzano (2011) noted that creating parent and community partnerships with schools to collaboratively manage student behavior was one of the first steps toward creating a safer school. Schools could work closely with others in the community to help instill ethical characteristics and encourage the development of ethical decision-making in all members of a society. In the context of cyber ethics and character development, the core values of home and school cultures need to overlap, and parents, educators, and community members have a responsibility to understand what it means to be a respectful citizen who is capable of making wise, ethical decisions both online and off (Ribble & Bailey, 2007; Ribble, 2012).

Social Learning Theory

According to Bandura's social learning theory, patterns of behavior are often learned directly from observing and modeling after others (1976). For example, if adults take a little pause before posting a rude comment online and use the rationale that it is their right to freedom of speech, it comes as no surprise when youth follow suit. Adults have the responsibility to be consistent models of appropriate behavior (Baum, 2005). However, parents and educators vary in their own knowledge and understanding of technology, and of how to use it safely and respectfully.

There is a growing concern for parents, teachers, and school staff to be on the same page when it comes to children's safety online (Keengwe et al., 2012). As educators integrate more technology into the classroom, Baum (2005) presumed that students would continue to partake in poor judgment when it comes to using the Internet and other digital devices. Therefore, he suggested that adults have the responsibility to be consistent models of appropriate online and offline behavior.

Social-Emotional Learning

As humans, we require social contact to live, even in an online world (Gorry, 2009). Yet, in a rapidly growing digital society, social contact has started to mean experiencing less physical interactions in face-to-face contexts, and more time socializing *virtually* behind the screens of computers, cell phones, and other digital devices. The Internet and other popular digital media tools have reinvented and redefined what relationships are and how people choose to interact with one another.

Empathy and social-emotional skills are important factors for healthy child development (Feng et al., 2004). In Goleman's (2005) *Emotional Intelligence*, he concluded that people who are able to accurately read and understand the feelings of others through nonverbal cues, like reading voice tones, gestures, and facial expressions are simply more emotionally adjusted, better liked, and overall more successful than those who do not have these intuitive interpersonal skills. On the flip side, Volbrecht et al. (2007) stated that children who lack a sense of empathy are more disposed to aggressive or antisocial behavior than children who have developed empathy. And, the potential risk for those children to commit aggressive acts against peers is increased exponentially (Dobrich & Dranoff, 2003).

Elias (2010) posited that we can create safe learning environments, decrease discipline problems, increase academic performance, produce effective members of society, and reduce such problems as cheating, bullying, and violence by including social-emotional learning and character development programs in our schools. The development of social-emotional competencies highly influences a child's overall wellbeing and can strengthen his or her success in numerous areas of life (i.e., social, academic, physical, mental) (Cohen, 2006). Internet safety and digital citizenship encompass far more than teaching online etiquette and manners to technology users and include many tenets of social-emotional learning. The Collaborative for Academic, Social, and Emotional Learning (CASEL, 2015) posited five SEL competencies: *self-awareness, self-management, social awareness, relationship skills*, and *responsible decision-making*.

Framing Online Digital Citizenship

In addressing several prominent citizenship programs in the United Kingdom, Pykett et al. (2010) applied Butler's theory of performativity and provided a method by which citizenship and its acts can be removed from political and academic rhetoric, "which assume that there is a convincing universal essence that makes for a good citizen" (p. 535). Their analysis highlighted several characteristics of good, active citizens: possessing certain virtues oriented primarily to the collective good of the community; respecting the rights and freedoms of others as they pursue their own interests; seeking and defending of social and economic equality; living sustainably and encouraging the same in social and political institutions; and working toward new forms of inclusion and recognition.

Kant believed that individuals should act based on moral self-constraint founded on reason instead of inclination or impulse (Wilson & Denis, 2018). Ultimately, Kant argued that an action is "right" if it could coexist with everyone else's freedoms. We find, however, that not everyone online possesses the perfect ethical imperative that Kant describes. Hume, on the other hand, contended that human morality and behavior are guided by sentiment and the need to feel pleasure from our actions. We experience from our personal judgments approval and disapproval and continuously adjust our sentiments to attain more approval. Hume maintained that individuals seek greater resemblance of his or her sentiments to others, increasing sympathy, and thereby attaining more contiguity to others. Yet in an online world, it is often difficult for users to observe the effects of their online actions. We find that because constructive feedback in online forums is often scarce or inconsistent, negative online behaviors are observed and replicated rather than avoided.

Further complicating matters is that digital citizens are socialized by peers, and not by the generations before them who more or less understand rules and regulations, right from wrong, and good from bad. With a lack of foundational levels of understanding and awareness of what digital citizenship is and what it should look like in terms of appropriate and inappropriate online behavior, it creates a humanistic problem worth investigating (Hollandsworth et al., 2011).

Digital Programs in the Asia-Pacific

However, where there are numerous programs in the United Kingdom and other western nations, studies and programs in the Asia-Pacific region are less prevalent. Several intervention programs to increase digital literacy have been implemented across the region (United Nations Educational, Scientific and Cultural Organization [UNESCO], 2015) by governments, nonprofit organizations, and private industry. Some programs include Malaysia's CyberSAFE and Klik Dengan Bijak (Click Wisely), Australia's Enhancing Online Safety for Children Act 2015, and Singapore's Inter-Ministry Cyber Wellness Steering Committee. The Asia-Pacific region, being of a wide geographical area with some of the most diverse cultures, languages, and ethnicities, represented six of the top 20 countries that ranked high on the ICT Development Index as well as the four of the least developed ICT-developed countries (UNESCO, 2016). In the UNESCO report, over 39% of households in the Asia-Pacific region were reported having access to the Internet in 2015 with 42.3% of people having mobile broadband subscriptions. In his work in Asian nation states, Michael Searson (2013) looked at the various policies through information communication technologies (ICT) to promote digital literacy and children's safe and responsible use of ICT. Additionally, Searson sought to better understand the challenges in implementing those programs. Some countries developed policies at the central level while others developed policies and programs in partnership with ministries of education, agencies, and other stakeholders. The more partners, the more complex.

Twenty two of the 46 member states in the Asia-Pacific region participated in the UNESCO 2014 survey on digital literacy and digital citizenship. In looking at four factors to support digital citizenship for students—a national agency to coordinate efforts, a national budget allocation, a national research program, an assessment program—responses to the survey indicated that more than half of the respondents indicated not having a research program nor an assessment program. Several responding member states did indicate having all four support factors in place; those member states were Brunei, Malaysia, New Zealand, People's Republic of China, and Singapore. However, what emerged was an understanding that the in-depth studies on digital citizenship in the European Union were not happening in the Asia-Pacific region (UNESCO, 2015).

We encourage scholars to examine the influence of the Internet on the values of citizenship in Asia-Pacific regions to consider how digital technology has redefined citizenship and civic contributions; compare the newly defined face-to-face and online personas; reflect on how adults can provide ethical guidance, and values of citizenship and engagement in young children online; and probe the aspects of the Internet that are perceived to affect a person's social capital in terms of a sense of community. As stated earlier, we believe research on how the Internet has influenced and changed interactions in communities in which we physically live and the communities and in which we might interact is important. It is our aim that addressing these inquiries in the Asia-Pacific can help inform the discussion about the influence that the Internet has on society and the evolution of the sense of citizenship in a digital space.

References

Al-Rafee, S., & Cronan, T. P. (2006). Digital piracy: Factors that influence attitude toward behavior. *Journal of Business Ethics, 63*(3), 237–259. https://doi.org/10.1007/s10551-005-1902-9.

Bandura, A. (1976). *Social learning theory.* https://www.thriftbooks.com/w/social-learning-theory_albert-bandura/248729/.

Baum, J. J. (2005). Cyberethics: The new frontier. *TechTrends, 49*(6), 54–55.

Bearden, S. M. (2016). *Digital citizenship: A community-based approach.* Corwin Press.

Berson, M., Berson, I., Desai, S., & Falls, D. (2008). *The role of electronic media in decision-making and risk assessment skill development in young children.* Presented at the Society for Information Technology and Teacher Education International Conference, Las Vegas, NV.

Bronfenbrenner, U. (1981). *The ecology of human development: Experiments by nature and design.* Cambridge, MA: Harvard University Press.

Cohen, J. (2006). Social, emotional, ethical, and academic education: Creating a climate for learning, participation in democracy, and well-being. *Harvard Educational Review, 76*(2), 201–237. https://doi.org/10.17763/haer.76.2.j44854x1524644vn.

Collaborative for Academic, Social, and Emotional Learning. (2015). *2015 CASEL guide: Effective social and emotional learning programs – Middle and high school edition.* Chicago, IL. http://secondaryguide.casel.org/casel-secondary-guide.pdf.

Dobrich, W., & Dranoff, S. (2003). *Can we stop sexual harassment and violence in middle school?* (Unpublished Paper). Rutgers University.

DuFour, R., & Mattos, M. (2013). How do principals really improve schools? *Educational Leadership, 70*(7), 34–40.

Elias, M. (2010). Character education: Better students, better people. *Education Digest: Essential Readings Condensed for Quick Review, 75*(7), 47–49.

Epstein, J. L. (1987). Toward a theory of family-school connections: Teacher practices and parent involvement. In K. Hurrelmann, F. Kaufmann, & F. Losel (Eds.), *Social intervention: Potential and constraints* (pp. 121–136). New York: DeGruyter.

Epstein, J. L. (2010). School/family/community partnerships: Caring for the children we share. *Phi Delta Kappan, 92*(3), 81–96. https://doi.org/10.1177/003172171009200326.

Feng, J., Lazar, J., & Preece, J. (2004). Empathy and online interpersonal trust: A fragile relationship. *Behaviour & Information Technology, 23*(2), 97–106. https://doi.org/10.1080/01449290310001659240.

Goleman, D. (2005). *Emotional intelligence: 10th anniversary edition; Why it can matter more than IQ.* https://www.barnesandnoble.com/w/emotional-intelligence-daniel-goleman/1125053411.

Gorry, G. A. (2009, August 31). Empathy in the virtual world. *The Chronicle of Higher Education.* https://www.chronicle.com/article/Empathy-in-the-Virtual-World/48180.

Hickey, M. G. (2002). Why did I get an "A" in citizenship?': An ethnographic study of middle school students' emerging concepts of citizenship. *Journal of Social Studies Research, 26*(2).

Holdsworth, N. (2007). Spaces to play/playing with spaces: Young people, citizenship and Joan Littlewood. *Research in Drama Education, 12*(3), 293–304.

Hollandsworth, R., Dowdy, L., & Donovan, J. (2011). Digital citizenship in K-12: It takes a village. *TechTrends: Linking Research and Practice to Improve Learning, 55*(4), 37–47. https://doi.org/10.1007/s11528-011-0510-z.

Howe, N., & Strauss, W. (1991). *Generations: The history of America's future, 1584 to 2069* (1st ed.). https://www.amazon.com/Generations-History-Americas-Future-1584/dp/0688119123.

Keengwe, J., Schnellert, G., & Mills, C. (2012). Laptop initiative: Impact on instructional technology integration and student learning. *Education and Information Technologies, 17,* 137–146. https://doi.org/10.1007/s10639-010-9150-8.

Liau, A. K., Khoo, A., & Hwaang, P. (2005). Factors influencing adolescent's engagement in risky internet behavior. *CyberPsychology & Behavior, 8*(6), 513–520.

Madhani, A., & Yu, R. (2015, November 12). Missouri controversy highlights academia's free speech struggle. *USA Today.* https://www.usatoday.com/story/news/2015/11/12/missouri-yale-campus-speech-first-amendment/75600646/.

Martinez, M. (2015, November 9). Colorado sexting scandal: High school faces felony investigation. *CNN.* https://www.cnn.com/2015/11/07/us/colorado-sexting-scandal-canon-city/index.html.

Marzano, R. J. (2011). Relating to students: It's what you do that counts. *Educational Leadership, 68*(6), 82.

Millman, C., Whitty, M., Winder, B., Trent, N., & Griffiths, M. D. (2012). Perceived criminality of cyber-harassing behaviors among undergraduate students in the United Kingdom. *International Journal of Cyber Behavior, Psychology and Learning (IJCBPL), 2*(4), 49–59. https://doi.org/10.4018/ijcbpl.2012100104.

Mossberger, K., Tolbert, C. J., & McNeal, R. S. (2007). *Digital citizenship: The internet, society, and participation.* MIT Press.

Mueller, J., & Wood, E. (2012). Patterns of beliefs, attitudes, and characteristics of teachers that influence computer integration. *Education Research International.* https://doi.org/10.1155/2012/697357.

Nguyen, T. T., & Mark, L. (2014). Cyberbullying, sexting, and online sharing: A comparison of parent and school faculty perspectives. *International Journal of Cyber Behavior, Psychology, and Learning, 4*(1), 76–86. https://doi.org/10.4018/ijcbpl.2014010106.

Nguyen, T. T. (2011). School faculty perspectives about Internet-safety youth behavior online. In C. D. Maddux (Ed.), *Research highlights in technology and teacher education 2011* (pp. 181–188). Society for Information Technology and Teacher Education.

Oxley, C. (2010, October). *Digital citizenship: Developing an ethical and responsible online culture.* Presented at The School Library Association of Queensland and the International Association of School Librarianship Conference Incorporating the International Forum on Research in School Librarianship, Brisbane, Queensland, Australia.

Paul, A. M. (2015, November 11). The Yale controversy is really about belonging. *Time.* https://time.com/4108632/yale-controversy-belonging/.

Prensky, M. (2001). Digital natives, digital immigrants. *On the Horizon, 9*(5), 1–6.

Pykett, J., Saward, M., & Schaefer, A. (2010). Framing the good citizen. *The British Journal of Politics and International Relations, 12*(4), 523–538. https://journals.sagepub.com/doi/10.1111/j.1467-856X.2010.00424.x.

Ribble, M., & Bailey, G. (2007). *Digital citizenship in schools.* Washington, DC: International Society for Technology in Education.

Ribble, Mike. (2012). Digital citizenship for educational change. *Kappa Delta Pi Record, 48*(4), 148–151.

Rubin, B. C. (2007). "There's still not justice": Youth civic identity development amid distinct school and community contexts. *Teachers College Record, 109*(2), 449–481.

Santo, C. A., Ferguson, N., & Trippel, A. (2010). Engaging urban youth through technology: The Youth Neighborhood Mapping Initiative. *Journal of Planning Education and Research, 30*(1), 52–65. https://doi.org/10.1177/0739456X10366427.

Searson, M. (2013). Mobile devices as disruptive tools for learning. In R. McBride & M. Searson (Eds.), *Proceedings of SITE 2013—Society for information technology & teacher education international conference* (pp. 3786–3788). Association for the Advancement of Computing in Education (AACE). https://www.learntechlib.org/primary/p/48700/.

Sheldon, S. B., & Epstein, J. L. (2002). Improving student behavior and school discipline with family and community involvement. *Education and Urban Society, 35*(1), 4–26.

Short, J., Williams, E., & Christie, B. (1976). *The social psychology of telecommunications.* Wiley.

Stephens, J. M., Young, M. F., & Calabrese, T. (2007). Does moral judgment go offline when students are online? A comparative analysis of undergraduates' beliefs and behaviors related to conventional and digital cheating. *Ethics and Behavior, 17*(3), 233–254. https://doi.org/10.1080/10508420701519197.

Syvertsen, A. K., Wray-Lake, L., Flanagan, C. A., Osgood, D. W., & Briddell, L. (2011). Thirty year trends in U.S. adolescents' civic engagement: A story of changing participation and educational differences. *Journal of Research on Adolescence, 21*(3), 586–594. https://doi.org/10.1111/j.1532-7795.2010.00706.x.

Technology Counts 2015: Learning the digital way—Education week. (2015, June 10). *Education Week.* https://www.edweek.org/ew/toc/2015/06/11/.

Thurlow, C., & Bell, K. (2009). Against technologization: Young people's new media discourse as creative cultural practice. *Journal of Computer-Mediated Communication, 14*(4), 1038–1049. https://doi.org/10.1111/j.1083-6101.2009.01480.x.

United Nations Educational, Scientific and Cultural Organization. (2015). Fostering digital citizenship through safe and responsible use of ICT: A review of current status. *Asia and the Pacific as of December 2014* (pp. 1–72).

United Nations Educational, Scientific and Cultural Organization. (2016). *A policy review: Building digital citizenship in Asia-Pacific through safe, effective and responsible use of ICT* (p. 118). https://bangkok.unesco.org/content/policy-review-building-digital-citizenship-asia-pacific-through-safe-effective-and.

Volbrecht, M. M., Lemery-Chalfant, K., Aksan, N., Zahn-Waxler, C., & Goldsmith, H. H. (2007). Examining the familial link between positive affect and empathy development in the second year. *The Journal of Genetic Psychology, 168*(2), 105–129. https://doi.org/10.3200/GNTP.168.2.105-130.

Waters, S. K., Cross, D. S., & Runions, K. (2009). Social and ecological structures supporting adolescent connectedness to school: A theoretical model. *Journal of School Health, 79*(11), 516–524. https://doi.org/10.1111/j.1746-1561.2009.00443.

Wellman, B., & Gulia, M. (1999). Net-surfers don't ride alone: Virtual communities as communities. In B. Wellman (Ed.), *Networks in the global village life in contemporary communities* (pp. 331–366). https://doi.org/10.4324/9780429498718-11.

Wilson, E. E., & Denis, L. (2018). Kant and Hume on morality. In E. N. Zalta (Ed.), *The Stanford encyclopedia of philosophy* (Summer 2018 Edition). https://plato.stanford.edu/archives/sum2018/entries/kant-hume-morality/.

Yee, N., Bailenson, J. N., Urbanek, M., Chang, F., & Merget, D. (2007). The unbearable likeness of being digital: The persistence of nonverbal social norms in online virtual environments. *CyberPsychology & Behavior, 10*(1), 115–121. https://doi.org/10.1089/cpb.2006.9984.

Zhao, S., Grasmuck, S., & Martin, J. (2008). Identity construction on Facebook: Digital empowerment in anchored relationships. *Computers in Human Behavior, 24*(5), 1816–1836. https://doi.org/10.1016/j.chb.2008.02.012.

Zhao, Y., & Frank, K. A. (2003). Factors affecting technology uses in schools: An ecological perspective. *American Educational Research Journal, 40*(4), 807–840. https://doi.org/10.3102/00028312040004807.

Chapter 4
Some Reflections on the Evolution and the Role of the Environmental Education

Dennis Nohemí De La Toba

Abstract Undoubtedly, environmental education plays a fundamental role in building and putting into practice human development strategies that allow raising the quality of life of our towns and cities. Environmental education must be an integrating factor of intellectual and collective development, related to the needs of communities and to the quality of life of all people. In this sense, environmental education is considered as education for the organization, for political action, for social and cultural progress. It is a permanent process that requires profound changes in the ways of educating a strategy and an environmental education program that challenge a human society alienated by a social system. The aim should be to act on the origins of the environmental problems, not only their consequences, combining strategies that articulate economic, political, and cultural issues. In this sense, the aim of this chapter is to reflect on the evolution of environmental education as a concept and a field of action and to share some reflections on its role and implications as a tool to foster environmental protection, social inclusion, and sustainable development. In our opinion, environmental education is crucial for the transformational change of the current development model.

Introduction

Environmental education as an institutionalized concept emerged in the 70s practically oriented toward the sustainable development and the implementation of Agenda 21 of the United Nations Environment Program (UNEP). The projects and tasks to be carried out until the twenty-first century show that the environmental education is crucial for promoting sustainable development and will allow expanding the capacity of citizens to address environmental and development issues.

At global scale, it is accepted that the environmental aspects should be incorporated as a fundamental part of learning in the different educational schemes. The purpose is to modify citizens' attitudes through knowledge, analysis, and evaluation

---

D. N. De La Toba (✉)
Ministry of Health, Consultant in Environmental Education, La Paz, Mexico

© The Author(s), under exclusive license to Springer Nature Singapore Pte Ltd. 2021
J. E. Rangel Delgado and A. Ivanova Boncheva (eds.), *Knowledge Society and Education in the Asia-Pacific*, SpringerBriefs in Education,
https://doi.org/10.1007/978-981-16-2333-2_4

of environmental problems with a sustainable development approach. This could be performed through formal education promoted by official educational institutions, as well as through non-formal one, created by civil society and communication media.

The current scenario is different from the one that existed in the 70 s and 80 s of the last century, when environmental education began to be promoted in a more systematic way. That´s why, nowadays, we can notice a new stage marked by less federal, state, and municipal initiatives and more activity of the civil society organizations. Nevertheless, the issue of environmental education has been strengthening and enriching discussions within interdisciplinary research, pedagogy, complexity, and the development of critical thinking, social transformation and the transversality of the educational-environmental processes.

Undoubtedly, environmental education plays a fundamental role in building and putting into practice human development strategies that allow raising the quality of life of our towns and cities.

Environmental education must be an integrating factor of intellectual and collective development, related to the needs of communities and to the quality of life of all people. In this sense, environmental education is considered as education for the organization, for political action, for social and cultural progress. It is a permanent process that requires profound changes in the ways of educating a strategy and an environmental education program that challenges a human society alienated by a social system. The aim should be to act on the origins of the environmental problems, not only their consequences, combining strategies that articulate economic, political, and cultural issues.

The multiple objectives and functions of the environmental education explore in detail and permanently, together with other disciplines, the relationships between human societies and nature to turn them into formative findings, which gives meaning to the need for an environmental pedagogy with visible results of action and social mobility that generates environmental benefits for all.

In this sense, the aim of this chapter is to reflect on the evolution of environmental education as a concept and a field of action and to share some reflections on its role and implications as a tool to foster environmental protection, social inclusion and sustainable development. In our opinion, the environmental education is crucial for the transformational change of the current development model.

Evolution of the Environmental Education: Concepts and Approaches

The starting point for understanding the advances in educational changes and the challenges that the knowledge society and globalization have imposed is the Delors Report (UNESCO, 1996) and the resolutions of the World Conference in Paris1(1998). The general principle of education today is education for life, based on the four pillars of education of the Delors Report:

1. *Learn to know.* It is the encounter of humanity with science and technology, that is, the interacting of the human with nature and society. The knowledge and understanding allow the human to make sense of his existence as an intellectual being.
2. *Learn to do.* This not only involves material work, but also implies mastering the cognitive and informative dimensions in production systems.
3. *Learn to live together, learn to live with others.* It implies the ability to understand the sense of coexistence, of collective construction, of the importance of the other and that, we are involved in the life of our environment and our survival depends on everyone.
4. *Learn to be.* Reencounter with yourself; fully develop all capacities as being integral, social, political, cultural, and economic being.

In this space of ideas, education is considered as a process and the school as the institution that generates the means to provide the knowledge, skills, and motivations necessary to train sensitive, conscious, and prepared people to interpret the world and act according to the changing circumstances. That´s why, the school can´t be the only center capable of training for life, but different kinds of knowledge and spaces must be intertwined to achieve comprehensive training.

The role of the environmental education is to build an integrated and articulated context, where the human being begins to analyze the situation of the planet due to the environmental crisis. He begins to question the growth model and its negative impact on the environment. Always, the human species have interacted with the environment and have modified it. However, what makes the current situation especially worrying is the acceleration of these modifications, and the massive and global nature of their consequences. Therefore, it is necessary to understand the development model and its neoliberal economic policy, globalization, and the crisis of civilization that the planet is going through, in order to understand the environmental dynamics.

Today, environmental problems no longer are independent of each other, but rather are elements that are interrelated. The new reality is different from the simple accumulation of all the negative impacts; it is more complex with multiple faces that manifest in its global nature. That´s why we must study the different social constructs of each culture on the environment, and explains the roles acquired by the different agents that intervene in the conception and management of the environment.

For this reason, environmental education is a social practice in permanent construction that aims to provide values, strategies, and knowledge appropriate to each sector of the population, to respond to the needs and contingencies of the complex transitions of our time. Thus, environmental education increases the awareness and knowledge of citizens on environmental issues or problems. By doing so, it provides the communities and the policymakers with the tools to make informed decisions and perform responsible action.

Maldonado (2005) analyzed the need to convert environmental education as a social tool within the educational process for the construction of a particular and collective conscience. This is a necessary tool to stimulate and execute educational, cultural, social processes under an environmentalist behavior, and orient the political and economic demands of the world's population in a sustainable way.

Viesca (2003) pointed out that an educational program cannot be the articulating axis of community actions to promote the required change processes, since in community development projects the best articulating axis for social change has been the social organization. That´s why, the field research must perform environmental education activities that meet the substantive needs of social groups and their relationships with the environment. In this way, research and practice in environmental education can play an essential role in personal, social, and environmental change (De La Toba, 2010).

Conceptualization and Ways to Address Environmental Education

In this part, we present a brief synthesis of the events and contributions that put into discussion on international level the environmental issues and environmental education in particular, from different perspectives and context. The purpose is to offer an integrated set of the most relevant elements that compose a coherent and global framework for the environmental education.

Environmental education emerged in the 1970s as a necessary and urgent alternative to modify human behavior. The aim was to solve and prevent problems caused by the impact of human activities on biophysical systems. Efforts in education were directed toward the proposal of pedagogical methods focused on problem-solving and the development of skills for environmental management, within the framework of scientific and technological education (Barraza, 2000).

The Stockholm Conference held in Sweden in 1972 was the world's first global environment forum. The problem generated by the prevailing development model in ecological terms was discussed on international level. The Conference highlighted also the marked differences between poor countries and developed countries, the excessive expansion of the industry, and the accelerated population growth.

During this international meeting, the United Nations Environment Program (UNEP) was created, an institution responsible for promoting and developing global policies on environmental issues (Cruces, 1997).

In Stockholm, the approach was a warning about the effects that human action can have on the material environment. The change in development styles or international relations was not discussed, but rather the correction of environmental problems that arise from current development styles or their environmental and social deformations.

Motivated by continued concern about environmental deterioration, in 1975 the United Nations Educational, Scientific and Cultural Organization (UNESCO), and the United Nations Environment Program (UNEP) decided to convene the international meeting in Belgrade, Serbia (former Yugoslavia). During this meeting, the role of education was considered as crucial to generate changes, through knowledge, attitudes, and values that can affront the environmental problems in the world.

As a result, the Belgrade Charter was constituted and adopted the agenda to establish basic guidelines, objectives, and goals of environmental education oriented to achieve a better quality of life for current and future generations. The need to reconsider the term "development" conceptually arises, being the environmental education the propitious tool to generate a new ethic in human–nature relationships (Zabala & García, 2008).

A continuous and permanent process of education must exist at all levels and in all educational modalities. It must apply an interdisciplinary, historical approach, with a global point of view, attending to regional differences and considering all development and growth from an environmental perspective.

In this sense, the principles of environmental education consider the environment as a totality where the human being and the ecological, economic, technological, social, legislative, cultural, and aesthetic issues converge. An interdisciplinary and historical approach must be applied to promoting cooperation in solving environmental problems.

The goal of environmental action is to improve ecological relationships: of humans with nature and of humans with each other. The environmental education intends to make the world population aware of the environment and have the knowledge, skills, attitudes, motivations, and wishes necessary to work individually and collectively in the search for solutions to current problems and to prevent those that may arise.

The main objectives of the environmental education are the following:

- awareness-raising to become conscious of everyday problems;
- knowledge acquisition to develop a critical understanding of reality;
- attitudes to promote social values and greater active participation in the protection and enhancing of the environment;
- capacities building to provide the necessary skills in problem-solving;
- evaluation capacity to provide an objective evaluation of the actions carried out in social, ecological, political, and educational aspects;
- participation capacity to adopt measures in solving environmental problems (Zabala & García, Op. cit.).

Another important event in 1977 was the Declaration of the Tbilisi Intergovernmental Conference on environmental education (UNESCO-PNUMA, 1977). This marked a huge advance with the agreement to incorporate environmental education into education systems, at all educational levels and within the framework of formal and non-formal education. The conclusions determined that it was not enough to raise awareness, but also to modify attitudes, provide new knowledge and criteria, as well as promote citizen participation in solving the problems. That meant to make a different education, outside the traditional schemes and based on action with a global vision. It was also pointed out that the media have a great responsibility to put their enormous resources at the service of the educational mission.

In the 80s, the concepts were oriented mainly to the transmission of environmental information (Barraza, 2001). This caused a polarization toward a single area of human development: the cognitive domain, which caused a deficiency in the levels of awareness and participation. The emphasis was on acquiring environmental knowledge (educating about the environment) and the predominant teaching method was based on data collection and receptive and passive learning.

In this decade, the International Congress on Environmental Education and Training was held in Moscow, USSR in 1987, convened by UNESCO and UNEP. A work document was created with the purpose of reviewing the environmental education policies suggested in Tbilisi, but, in addition, a strategic plan on Environmental Education and Training was proposed.

According to Muñoz (1994), among the actions proposed in this document are: access to information; research and experimentation; educational programs and teaching materials; personnel training; technical and vocational education; education and information to the public; general university education; specialist training; international and regional cooperation.

However, in this document, the main cause of the environmental problem was attributed to poverty. An absence of analysis and criticism of the underlying problem and the consideration of the context of current dominant development must be pointed out.

During the 1990s, environmental education entered a conceptual crisis, closely associated with the many problems raised by its practice. This practice emphasized the promotion of activities and caused an imbalance between doing for doing and understanding what needs to be done (Barraza, s/f).

In 1992, the Earth Summit in Rio de Janeiro, Brazil, issued several documents, among which it is important to highlight Agenda 21, which contains a series of tasks to be carried out until the twenty-first century. In the Agenda, Chapter 36 is dedicated to the promotion of education, training, and awareness. It establishes three program areas: The reorientation of education toward sustainable development, the raising of public awareness, and the promotion of training (Zabala & García, 2008).

Parallel to the Earth Summit, the Rio 92 Global Citizen Forum was held. This Forum approved 33 treaties; among them is the Treaty of Environmental Education toward Sustainable Societies and Global Responsibility. It characterizes the Environmental Education as "an act for social transformation, not neutral but political, and considers education as a permanent learning process based on respect for all forms of life." This Treaty issues 16 principles of education for the formation of sustainable societies and global responsibility. These recognize the education as a right of all, based on critical and innovative thinking, with a holistic perspective and aimed at addressing the causes of critical global issues and promoting democratic change.

The treaty clearly points out the scarce citizen participation and the destruction of traditional human values. It is urgent to modify the existing proposals that insist on continuing with the current development model.

Strictly speaking, the 1990s evaded the advance of the approach to environmental education and restricted it to actions motivated by citizen activism but lacking structure, meaning, and roots.

The Iberoamerican Congress of Environmental Education held in Guadalajara, Mexico in 1992 established that the environmental education is eminently political.

It was recognized its role as an essential instrument to achieve an environmentally sustainable and socially fair society. The environmental education contributes also to foster the social participation and community organization aimed at global transformations toward optimal quality of life and democracy that seeks the self-development of the person.

The important components in this sense are professionalization of environmental educators; training of citizenship and citizen participation; communication and community environmental education; education for conservation and tourism; education on human rights (Zabala & García, 2008).

At the beginning of the twenty-first century, the concept of environmental education was further restructured. It was linked to sustainability and human development. However, the conceptual limits and the environmental pedagogy needed more definition.

An important event held in the first decade of the twenty-first century was the declaration of the Decade of Education for Sustainable Development (DEDS), which began on January 1, 2005 and ended in December 2014. In the General Resolution is stated that the fundamental objective of the DEDS is "to encourage governments to include into the International Implementation Plan, the measures to apply in their respective educational systems, as well, as the strategies to include in their national development plans. The International Implementation Plan, published in 2006 stated that the general objective of the DEDS is to integrate the principles, values and practices inherent to the sustainable development in all aspects of education and learning."

Mexico signed this commitment in March 2005 and established a National Commitment for the Decade of Environmental Education for Sustainable Development. It led to the development of plans for environmental education in the different states of the country and of the Environmental Education Strategy for Sustainability in Mexico.

This Strategy was applied in the period 2006–2014, emphasizing the importance of designing and putting into practice processes that allow critical assessment of the implemented programs, projects, and experiences of Environmental Education for Sustainability. The government's public policy adopted the concept "Environmental Education for Sustainability," with an integrative approach in its actions, developed at local, state, and national levels.

Finally, we can observe that the concept of environmental education has evolved and undergone important changes during its brief history. It has matured from the biological, conservationist, systemic and integrative approaches to sustainability, developing an integrative and articulated transdisciplinary vision.

Environmental Education as an Instrument to Solve the Environmental Problems in a Globalized World

Environmental problems are the most difficult challenge facing humanity in the twenty-first century. They are primarily caused by the technology that prioritizes the use of natural assets for accumulation of capital concentrated in few hands.

The international community, governments, and citizens are becoming aware that the technological development that has made life comfortable can turn around and make it impossible. Pollution and conservation, which were conceptualized only of an environmental nature, become social problems linked to forms of organization, culture, and human values (Calvo & Gutiérrez, 2007).

The environmental problems that humanity has witnessed in recent decades proclaim the limit of the project of western civilization and its development model based on an economistic vision of the world. Thus, it announces the deep crisis of capitalism that has measured its progress only through "quantitative indicators and economic growth" (Sauvé et al., 2008).

This is why it becomes crucial to reveal the contradictions that have made this civilizing model unsustainable prevails. Gutiérrez (1999) mentions three main phenomena in the contradictions manifested by the expansion of the capitalist model: the increase in marginalization and poverty; the crisis of the human condition (or of existence), and the ecological crisis of the planet.

Two great scenarios emerge in the last decades of the twentieth century: the knowledge society and globalization. Both of them generate different processes that shape the social life in all its manifestations and have a drastic impact on the modification, both of educational paradigms and of the nature of work. In general terms, the knowledge society and the globalization process show a marked tendency toward homogenization (Malagón, 1999).

This increasingly pronounced trend undoubtedly shows that the polarization of knowledge has been instituted in a single way of seeing and operating things, that of mercantilist production and entrenched conventionality. From the point of view of culture, it can be said that the indiscriminate attack on national and regional cultures is very similar to what European civilizations did with the new world. In such a situation, education plays an important role in maintaining the roots of customs, regional and national traditions, in the face of the globalizing processes.

Despite the homogenization of culture, the Earth continues to be divided by cultural diversity, but shares the same accumulation system. As recognized by the Brundtland Report on Environment and Development in 1987, this is perhaps the most serious environmental problem in the contemporary world. The environmental impact of modern development is not only the effect of a simple technological development, but also the result of an accumulation system (Maya, 1995).

Therefore, it is not possible to analyze the contemporary environmental problems without analyzing the accumulation poles and consequently the exploitation or poverty poles. Angel Maya states that the fact that culture is increasingly homogenized does not mean, therefore, that modern society lives within the same conditions of satisfaction of its needs. The immense development of the quality of life in the rich countries has been achieved as a function of the exploitation of the resources of the poor countries and the subordination of their cultures. For this reason, the environmental problems are interdependent. They cannot be analyzed in isolation. The cultures therefore do not die of natural death, they are buried by accumulation flows.

Modern production systems continue to expand, contesting the rights of members of rural communities over their most productive lands and their most valuable resources. Therefore, the environmental crisis we are experiencing is a crisis of our civilization, "it is the crisis of an economic, technological and cultural model that has preyed on nature and denied alternate cultures." The environmental crisis is not ecological, but a social one, a result of a mechanistic view of the world that ignores the biophysical limits of nature and the lifestyles of different cultures (Pérez, s/f).

The threat of the environmental crisis is real, is located in the present, and ultimately does not respect borders or nations. Ecosystems, species, and cultures are threatened in one way or another. Education is an essential element of the global response to climate change. It helps young people understand and address the impact of global warming, encourages changes in their attitudes and behavior, and helps them adapt to climate change-related trends. Environmental education makes us reflect on it and therefore the environmental problems require a common solution. The current capitalist development model is contrary to the essence of community solutions, which limits the opportunity to face the emerging problems.

The Sustainable Development Goals (SDGs) adopted by the global community recognize the importance of education in achieving their targets by 2030. The Global Action Program (GAP) on Education for Sustainable Development (ESD), which ran from 2015 to 2019, aimed to generate and scale-up ESD and to accelerate progress toward sustainable development (UNESCO, 2015). Through its Climate Change Education for Sustainable Development program, UNESCO aims to make climate change education a more central and visible part of the international response to climate change. The program aims to help people understand the impact of global warming today and increase "climate literacy" among young people (UNESCO, 2010). It does this by strengthening the capacity of its Member States to provide quality climate change education; encouraging innovative teaching approaches to integrate climate change education in school and by raising awareness about climate change as well as enhancing non-formal education programs through media, networking, and partnerships.

As Barbero and Cortés (2005) emphasize: "We are therefore facing a structurally fractured society, in which the divorce between state and society becomes more and more visible and deeper every day. In the vast majority of countries, the state is acting by the rules of game set by the International Monetary Fund, the World Trade Organization and the World Bank, then by the demands for development of their own societies. In Latin America the states are not only reduced and rather impotent, but also incapable and incoherent, and therefore the society degrades day by day as a result of the growth of exclusion."

Given the scheme that the world is like this, we cannot stay with the feeling that it will not change but must rather analyze what we should do or how we should act in a globalized world. In order to establish some of the parameters that this transformation would require, we will follow the line of ideas of Bifani (2007, p. 1997), who considers that the development is existing only when it increases quantitatively but above all qualitatively the wellbeing of all and the respect for ecosystems and the life forms that they support.

Environmental education has been a permanent process in order to make individuals and society in general aware of their environment and acquire knowledge, skills, and values; that allows them to develop a positive role, both individually and collectively toward protecting the environment and improving the quality of human life (Barbero, 2011; Covas, 2004). Consequently, the formation of environmental attitudes and values, the development of critical thinking, and citizen participation in a consistent, profound, and active way, can only be achieved through education.

Therefore, the solution points in one direction: the deconstruction of the current development model. However, how to transform the civilization model from the school? Undoubtedly an important question that does not denote solutions, at least in the short term. To have real tangible and visible results, we must carry out a work in school and in community that allows us to have answers on how to generate satisfactory results.

How can we advance in school will depend on how problems are thought, what dimensions of the crisis are prioritized, and, the aspirations of the school to perform a pedagogical guide to the practice.

Conclusions

As a conclusion, we will outline some reflections to point out the needs and considerations lacking both in the discourse and in the practice of environmental education, in any context and field of development.

After 47 years of environmental education, very important advances have been made in its conceptualizing and positioning. However, it is still under construction, not only because of the methodologies that are evolving, but rather because it must reinvent itself according to the conditions of this dynamic world. The earth claims it.

Reflection 1. To solve a legitimate environmental education, it is necessary to break paradigms, transcend mental borders, understand the changing reality and be ready for individual change. We must act transversally and connect with the different social actors on state, municipal, and local level, on a vertical and horizontal axis; establish solid inter and intra institutional links with clear and dynamic objectives. This may consolidate the field of environmental education, recognizing in this sense, the capacity for self-management of localities, citizen participation, and regional identity.

Reflection 2. For environmental education to stop being a nice political and academic discourse, it is necessary to consolidate its action and its position, raise its economic budget and create a strong institutional framework: plans, programs, and strategies with real impact, and not just justification mechanisms for simulation.

Reflection 3. It is necessary to document the processes of change in the field of environmental education and reconsider the work of the environmental educator.

Reflection 4. The environmental education cannot generate change; but it can lay the foundations to promote it. A pedagogical political project must be produced that includes social and economic processes. The major problems to face are lack of budget, stagnation of programs, public policies that go in another direction, marginalized populations, environmental degradation, and population growth.

Reflection 5. The behavior of individuals is the most evident manifestation that there is a change of thought and the creation of a different consciousness. Therefore, it can be assumed that education is a constantly evolving process of social awareness that affects values through educational processes. Therefore, the role of the school is essential to trigger processes that promote such awareness.

Reflection 6. The training and updating processes are priority in the field of environmental education for teachers, promoters, and communicators that create learning communities allowing the exchange of experiences and promoting dialogue, and community organization. Thus, creating a multiplier effect to achieve an environmental culture and to develop more consolidated and continuous strategies in urban and rural communities.

Reflection 7. The environmental education must work based on the local reality and build the hope of its inhabitants. The aim is to train thinking and critical people that perform responsible actions toward social transformation.

Reflection 8. Education commits to form people who participate, who build and carry out a process of disengagement that allows the building of new knowledge, people committed to improving their environment and living space. This new education requires generating management processes that train for empowerment and self-management of people and communities.

Reflection 9. It is urgent to consider the environmental education as a public policy that integrates the efforts of the environmental, educational, and social development sectors that contribute to recovering and maintaining hope, that reminds us of the joy of living, that makes us recognize what has been done well and what has been done wrong, and do things better. It is a priority to regain confidence in the human being.

Reflection 10. The education must be diversified according to different contexts. In this educational proposal, an open system is required, which incorporates the different modalities of education: formal, non-formal, and informal to advance toward a different type of development.

Reflection 11. The persons must be educated to acquire knowledge that gives them autonomy, since they cannot participate jointly if they do not know themselves. This implies, therefore, to transform the educational processes in coherent, authentic, and reliable actions, where everyone assumes values based on dialogue, tolerance, participation, and respect for life, creativity, cooperation, co-responsibility, and solidarity.

Reflection 12. Build new ways of thinking, modify our behavior patterns, and organize to solve the problems, promote new forms of coexistence, rethink the traditional values, and live according to new values. Without the formation of better attitudes that differ from consumer society, it will be impossible to solve the serious environmental problems of our locality, country, and world.

Reflection 13. Facilitate the permanent participation of students in the activities that promote their integral development and strengthen the training of environmental promoters that favor their critical understanding of the environmental dimension.

Reflection 14. Sensitize communities to get involved in environmental educational and management processes, which allow them a critical and comprehensive understanding of their environmental reality—and its relationship with all areas of social, economic, political, cultural life—and improve their abilities to solve their problems.

Reflection 15. It is necessary to create links between institutions, civil society organizations, international organizations, and communities, based on cross-cutting programmatic axes that complement educational action and improve its efficiency and effectiveness.

Reflection 16. The sensitivity and culture of the society and the educational institutions is very low regarding the environmental issues (disinterest, apathy, and minimal commitment to environmental and educational problems in general). The population does not participate with its particular visions in the decisions and actions on the development due to top-down approaches to planning. Additional difficulties involving the population are unemployment, migration, addictions, and loss of values that lead to social disintegration. The programs and campaigns to disseminate environmental issues are discontinuous. Their teaching tools are often inadequate and do not reflect the social, cultural, and economic characteristics of each particular community or region.

Reflection 17. Promote the professional ethical training of environmental educators who participate in the three educational modalities: formal, non-formal and informal, with a cross-cutting approach, which concerns the environmental dimension. The adequate pedagogical management, both in rural and urban locations, will foster favorable attitudes to sustainable development and a better way of life.

Reflection 18. It is necessary to work with better management of textbooks, since the teaching of environmental topics is limited to isolated reflections on reality. Hence the need for the integration of the environmental and cultural context, as well as the daily practices of the students, which is very favorable for the understanding, knowledge, and appreciation of nature and the elements that make it up in the immediate environment and with which children and young people coexist in their daily lives and practices.

There is still a long way to go, there is an urgent need to transform this civilizational model through deep introspection under the awareness that all kinds of education must be environmental.

References

Barbero, G. J. M. (2011). La pertenencia en el horizonte de las nuevas tecnologías y de la sociedad de la comunicación. En M. Hopenhayn & A.Sojo (Comps.), *Sentido de pertenencia en sociedades fragmentadas. América Latina en una perspectiva global* (pp. 105). 1a ed. - Siglo Veintiuno Editores. Buenos Aires. Argentina.

Barbero, G. J. M., & Cortés, I. F. (2005). *Trabajo comunitario, organización y desarrollo Social.* Alianza Editorial, S. A. Madrid.

Barraza, L. (2000). *Educar para el futuro: en busca de un nuevo enfoque de investigación en educación ambiental* (pp. 253–260). Memorias Foro Nacional de Educación Ambiental. UAA, SEP y SEMARNAP.

Barraza, L. (2001). Environmental education in Mexican schools: A review at primary level. *Journal of Environmental Education., 32,* 31–36.

Barraza, L. (s/f). *Lineamientos de la educación ambiental en el Siglo XXI.* Centro de Investigaciones en Ecosistemas, UNAM. Michoacán, México.

Bifani, P. (2007). *Medio Ambiente y Desarrollo.* México: Editorial Universitaria, Guadalajara, Jal.

Calvo, S., & Gutiérrez, J. (2007). *El espejismo de la educación ambiental.* Editores Morata, S.L. Madrid, España.

Covas, A. O. (2004). *Educación ambiental a partir de tres enfoques: Comunitario, Sistémico e Interdisciplinario.* Diplomante en Dirección Científica, ISP "Pepito Tey"; Cuba.

Cruces, J. (1997). Etapas del discurso ambiental en el tema del desarrollo. Espacios, *18*(1). http://wwwrevistaespacios.com/a97v18n01/10971801.html.

De La Toba, D. (2010). *Límites y Posibilidades de la Educación Ambiental para la Organización y Participación Comunitaria en la Conservación de los Oasis Sudcalifornianos* (Master Dissertation). University of Guadalajara, Mexico.

Gutiérrez Rosete, J. G. (1999). Sustentabilidad, cultura y globalidad. En E. González Corona & I. García Rojas (Coords.), *Diversidad Cultural en la globalización* (pp. 52–64). Universidad de Guadalajara.

Malagón, P. L. A. (1999). Educación, Trabajo y Globalización: Una perspectiva desde la Universidad. *Educación Superior y Sociedad / IESAL / UNESCO., 10*(2), 29–52.

Maldonado, D. H. A. (2005). La educación ambiental como herramienta social. *Geoenseñanza, 10,* 61–67.

Maya, C. A. A. (1995). *La Fragilidad Ambiental de la Cultura.* Instituto de Estudios Ambientales. IDEA. Colombia: Editorial Universidad Nacional.

Muñoz Oraá, L. (1994). *Contribución a la Historia de la Educación Ambiental en Venezuela.* Guanare: UNELLEZ.

Pérez, P.V. (s/f). *Educación ambiental y cosmovisión de los pueblos originarios.* Unidad de Cultura Ambiental, Comisión Nacional del Medio Ambiente-CONAMA-, Región de Tarapacá, Chile.

Sauvé, L., Berryman, T., & Brunelle, R. (2008). Tres décadas de normatividad internacional para la educación ambiental: una crítica hermenéutica del discurso de Naciones Unidas. En: González Gaudiano, Edgar (Coord.), *Educación, medio ambiente y sustentabilidad* (pp. 55–73). México: Siglo XXI Editores.

UNESCO-PNUMA. (1977). *Declaración de la conferencia Intergubernamental de Tbilisi: Informe final.*

UNESCO. (1996). *La educación encierra un tesoro. Informe de la Comisión Internacional sobre la Educación para el Siglo XXI.* presidida por Jacques Delors. 1 ed. Santillana y la Organización. Madrid, España.

UNESCO. (2010). *Climate change education for sustainable development.* https://unesdoc.unesco.org/ark:/48223/pf0000190101/PDF/190101eng.pdf.multi.

UNESCO. (2015). *Global action programme on education for sustainable development (2015–2019).* https://en.unesco.org/globalactionprogrammeoneducation.

Viesca, A. M. (2003). Principales aportes de una investigación en educación ambiental realizada en el ámbito rural. *Tópicos en Educación Ambiental, 5*(13), 31–42.

Zabala, G., &García, M. (2008). Historia de la Educación Ambiental desde su discusión y análisis en los congresos internacionales. *Revista de Investigación, 32*(63).

Chapter 5
The Russia's Knowledge Society

José Ernesto Rangel Delgado and Ángel Licona Michel

Abstract This chapter is focused on science and technology social development space. This topic is timely and relevant to identify the human resources development policies in regions of rapid expansion of knowledge-based society, and especially in Northeast Asian Pacific countries where Russia is located. The study is centered on the formation of human resources to foster knowledge-based society, including public policy aspects related to achieve the equilibrium between demand and supply of well-educated human capital, and to foster knowledge, science, technology, and innovation. The hypothesis of this research is based on the lack of linkage between private sector, higher education, new technologies, and employment opportunities to reach equilibrium between demand and supply of graduates. Another important question refers to the congruence of those policies (active or passive), related to the specific characteristics of the country. To support this analysis, we use International Labor Organization (ILO) official data, and other digital information. Additionally, we analyze the opinions of key informants from different sectors of Russian society, including government, business, and academia.

Introduction

Better-trained and qualified human resources significantly increase productivity indexes and contribute to improved understanding among nations, based on increased tolerance and respect. Benefits of free trade are important because capably trained human capital substantially contributes to competitive development of industries and to improved standard of living of citizens. Well-designed and implemented public policies can effectively foster development, thus contributing to society's well-being.

J. E. Rangel Delgado (✉) · Á. Licona Michel
University of Colima, Villa de Álvarez, México
e-mail: erangel@ucol.mx

Á. Licona Michel
e-mail: almichel@ucol.mx

© The Author(s), under exclusive license to Springer Nature Singapore Pte Ltd. 2021
J. E. Rangel Delgado and A. Ivanova Boncheva (eds.), *Knowledge Society and Education in the Asia-Pacific*, SpringerBriefs in Education,
https://doi.org/10.1007/978-981-16-2333-2_5

However, often well-educated people are unemployed. This situation is common in the global economy in spite of the demand for more educated human resources. That's why this chapter is focused on science and technology social development space. This topic is timely and relevant to identify the human resources development policies in regions of rapid expansion of knowledge-based society, and especially in Northeast Asian Pacific countries where Russia is located.

The study is centered on the formation of human resources to foster knowledge-based society, including public policy aspects related to achieve the equilibrium between demand and supply of well-educated human capital, and to foster knowledge, science, technology, and innovation.

The hypothesis of this research is based on our previous work (Rangel & Ivanova, 2012; Rangel et al., 2018), related to the lack of linkage between private sector, higher education, new technologies, and employment opportunities to reach equilibrium between demand and supply of graduates.

Without a doubt, another important question refers to the congruence of those policies (active or passive), related to the specific characteristics of the country. To support this analysis, we use International Labor Organization (ILO) official data, and other digital information. Additionally, we analyze the opinions of key informants from different sectors of Russian society, including government, business, and academia.

The Knowledge-Based Society (KBS)

KBS has as precedent the Knowledge-Based Economy (KBE), two approaches that deserve a thoughtful and deep consideration. he Both concepts are closely related to other fundamental aspects for the harmonious and sustained development of Russia, such as the development of human resources, productivity, competitiveness, and social and economic stability.

The KBE concept was introduced by Organization for Economic Cooperation and Development (OECD), and adopted later by other international organizations to explain commerce and investment in a framework of global competitiveness. In this context, we must consider the different endowments of intellectual capital, that globally position the countries in the field of education, science, technology, inventions, and patents of general knowledge.

Therefore, the nowadays market is no longer that of goods and services based on raw materials, but still based on merchandise. This time the added value of goods and services is measured in terms of the amount of knowledge in the design, performance, placement on internet and the management of digital markets, as well as for the recognition of intellectual property to be commercialized in the different economies of the world. In this sense, the KBS emphasizes on a highly trained human resource, basis for all the processes for competitive production, whose final purpose is social welfare.

5 The Russia's Knowledge Society

This chapter presents a theoretical approach to the subject, to explain what is happening in Russia in this sector. First, we analyze the contributions of classical economics (Adam Smith), Gary Becker's theory of human capital, and Paul Romer's endogenous growth theory, as the main theoretical framework. These contributions are supported by the implicit approaches of business management theory of the United Nations Program and the Fourth Industrial Revolution (i4.0) that explain the relationship between economic growth, education, and society.

The classical economy, from the sixteenth to seventeenth centuries, highlighted education as a factor of economic growth. Smith (2007)stated that one part of a country's fixed capital consists of expertise acquired by the persons, and useful to all members of society. Improving the skill of a worker can be considered similar to enhance a business instrument that facilitates and shortens the work, and although it involves a certain cost, this is compensated by benefit. From this point of view, and from different perspectives, countries have seen education as a sufficient reason to ensure prosperity and well-being, and Russia has been no exception.

In addition, we can consider the Theory of Human Capital (HCT) fostering the economic endogenous theory (Romer, 1994). This HCT constitutes a paradigm that explains systemically the relationship between education, productivity, and income (Becker, 1983). It is based on the neoclassical school of economics and considers education as an investment performed by the individual, thus increasing his income in the future.

Those economic models were signaling the interest of accumulating human capital to increase the productivity of the individual, therefore, scientific and technological innovation and the emergence of new productive requirements that place the knowledge acquired through education and research, as a strategic factor for economic growth.

The HCT has led to the discussion of education, training, science, and technology policies within the economic politics of the countries, leading to proposals for human resource planning under assumptions related to workforce quality, and to production requirements. Likewise, it is considered that investment in education is required to support the economic growth, which promotes a fair distribution of benefits.

Following this brief theoretical route of construction of the KBS, we present the business management approach, which in regions such as Latin America, begins to see human capital, no longer as an object of expenditure, but as an object of investment (CEPAL-UNESCO, 1992). Therefore, it becomes possible for the private sector to subsidize schooling to form human capital and at the same time, turn the production into a means of learning. The basic assumption of this approach is that education, training, and technological innovation are fundamental to business success.

Thus, it is necessary to design the educational systems according to the framework of knowledge, skills, and attitudes that the competitive transformation of the different productive sectors demands, developing competitive advantages (Porter, 1999), so that countries and companies can create a pool of highly qualified personnel, investing resources for this purpose.

The increasing awareness of the strategic value of human capital for the competitive performance of companies, makes it possible to contribute to the strengthening of the links between the education sector and the resource training needs of companies. Thus, the business sector becomes a leading actor in the curricular design supporting the educational training and complementing the links to the work centers.

These theoretical approaches present solutions that directly link education with economic growth, but this is not enough for social purposes. They must also consider another sphere of action that refers to the creation of a positive social climate, and therefore to the achievement of socioeconomic stability, allowing the individuals active participation in the generation of science and technology based on socially accepted values. Since 1990, the human development approach of the United Nations Development Program represents an important tool to understand the role of education and its contribution to social equity. According to the concept of human development, the level of progress of a country is estimated based on three components that reflect the well-being of the population: longevity, purchasing power, and level of knowledge. A fundamental concern of Human Development is the quality of life of the people; thus, it assumes that investment in people increases their productivity, rejecting the idea that humans are only an instrument of production (Stiglitz & Greenwald, 2014).

That's why government investment and financing of education have to be performed in a clear and transparent way according to consistent objectives of human resource training, prioritizing their social character. Therefore, macroeconomic stabilization strategies should be articulated with educational policy and planning, as a comprehensive project in which any proposal for reactivation, consolidation, or innovation includes the benchmark for quantitative and qualitative characteristics of human resources training.

The business environment, the information and communication technology infrastructure, the innovation systems, the training of human resources, should be involved in networking as originally proposed by the OECD. In this context we could include other concepts in the discussion (sociology and management), such as the Knowledge Industry (Machlup, 1962); La societé post-industrielle (Touraine, 1969); the Coming of Post-Industrial Society (Bell, 1973); New Society of Organizations (Drucker, 1992); Network or information society (Castells, 2000a, b, c). All these concepts are evolving nowadays to explain the importance of knowledge in globalization (Dabat-Latrubesse & Rodriguez-Vargas, 2009), and in relation to the Fourth Industrial Revolution (Schuwab, 2016).

KBS strengthens with i4.0, where humans promote creativity and thinking to maintain market competitiveness, supporting new employment modalities. These new modalities focus mainly on human resource development facing the opportunities offered by i4.0, with an emphasis on requalification. At the same time, companies perform greater investment in education, training, and capacity building of workers. Important financing is oriented also to innovation, based on the advances of robotics and artificial intelligence for fruitful social dialogue. Three relevant elements are the basis for this dialogue: (a) The innate human ability to recognize the problem; (b) The innate human ability to explore alternatives, linked to science and technology, in particular to knowledge generation, and; (c) the human capacity to collaborate and communicate with bots to anticipate what they can do, avoiding to fall into a perverse dependency (Schuwab, 2016).

Thus, in each of the aforementioned theoretical approaches, there are assumptions that try to base the statements on the characteristics of the relationship between the public and private sectors to offer better conditions for development. On the one hand, exist the approaches of a quantitative order that don´t consider nor social variables; on the other hand, the approach of a less linear vision of development that includes aspects as quality of life, considering education, science, development, and technological innovation.

This theoretical chain articulation allows us to visualize a society in which education, science, and technology are based on knowledge without neglecting the qualitative aspects that an economy in transition like Russia implies.

What About Russia's KBS?

To interpret the KBS in Russia, we propose to use an analysis that considers the following indicators. Foreign Direct Investment that fosters an expansion of business over the period 1990–2018, limited by sanctions imposed by the west, which promote erratic behavior of the indicator, particularly from 2014. The sanctions by the west for the incorporation of Crimea, and the emergence of an economic policy focused on import substitution, which favors a domestic business environment. The information and communication technology infrastructure, innovation systems, the training of human resources and other aspects such as networking and the i4.0 impacting on the Federation, for the formation of an ad hoc knowledge society.

According to Fig. 5.1, the data on Foreign Direct Investment in Russia shows that between 1992 and 2003 the behavior of the indicator was one digit. During the following 10 years (between 2004 and 2014), the data rises to two digits rapidly until 2009, recovering notably from 2010 to 2013, and starting to lose relevance

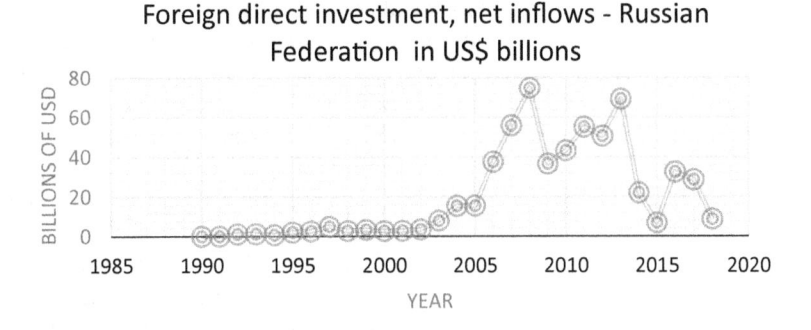

Fig. 5.1 Foreign direct investment, net inflows (USD billions) (*Source* World Bank [2020a])

Mobile celular sucription and internet use - Russian Federation

◆ Mobile cellular subscription (per 100 people)

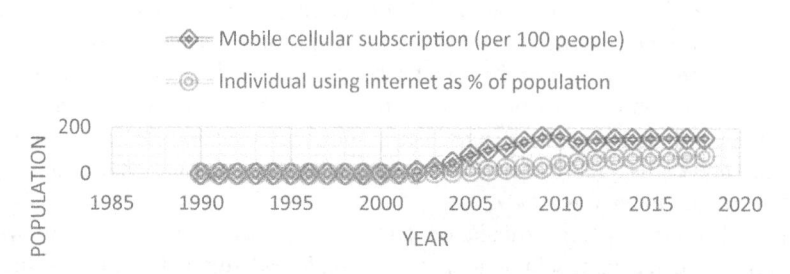

◎ Individual using internet as % of population

Fig. 5.2 Mobile subscription (per 100 people) and internet use (% of the population) (*Source* World Bank [2020b, c])

from 2014, due to the Crimea's issue, which is reflected in 2015. During 2016–2017, we can note a new recovery, declining the growth rate again in 2018. What we observe is that Foreign Direct Investment has not stopped flowing, according to data from the World Bank (2020a). In this way, Russia's connection with the outside world continues with vicissitudes, deteriorating, but without stopping, which in a way shows, on one hand, that the business environment continues favorable to the interests of foreign companies, complemented by a domestic production based on an economic policy of import substitution.

Figure 5.2 shows that KBS is reinforced by the degree of connectivity, expressed particularly by the number of cell phones per hundred inhabitants, and the use of the internet by the population, which has been high in the period. It is important to consider that the population inserts itself fast in the global community during 1990–2018, which, on the one hand, favors the opening of businesses. However, the sovereign internet was introduced, as a measure of control and security of the country in the face of possible cyber-attacks, and the assessment of a certain perverse effect caused by the excessive use of ICTs (Kurpatov, 2020; World Bank, 2020b, c).

However, Table 5.1 shows that contrary to the strengthening of a healthy KBS, Russia has substantially decreased the number of researchers per one million inhabitants. That means, according to the central definition of the KBS, that its global participation is constantly decreasing and that the possibilities of generating value are diminishing compared to the import substitution it faces due to the sanctions imposed by the West. The former combined with practices as inbreeding, lack of rigor, plagiarism, and limited international collaboration, according to the Report by the Commission created at the Academy of Sciences to investigate falsification in scientific research (Ruiz, 2020).

Likewise, according to the data in Table 5.1, Russia appears only in eighth place (below China, the United States, Japan, South Korea, the European Patent Office, Germany, and India) among the top 10 offices that received the highest number of patent applications in 2018 (WIPO, 2019). The country appears, as well as second for double-digit growth, among the five countries, in terms of counting industrial

5 The Russia's Knowledge Society

Table 5.1 Number of Researchers dedicated to research and development (per million people)

Year	Russia	USA	Japan	South Korea	China	Mexico
1996	3,796	3,136	4,874	2,173	438	208
1997	3,603	3,238	4,929	2,222	468	220
1998	3,342	3,404	5,135	1,985	383	211
1999	3,383	3,462	5,175	2,131	416	218
2000	3,459	3,493	5,078	2,287	542	219
2001	3,468	3,564	5,113	2,858	575	227
2002	3,388	3,649	4,871	2,956	624	298
2003	3,371	3,892	5,094	3,134	660	318
2004	3,316	3,787	5,099	3,221	705	371
2005	3,235	3,741	5,304	3,692	847	405
2006	3,240	3,806	5,333	4,090	921	329
2007	3,277	3,781	5,325	4,523	1,065	339
2008	3,154	3,937	5,108	4,798	1,185	331
2009	3,091	4,093	5,099	4,942	852	372
2010	3,088	3,890	5,103	5,330	891	328
2011	3,124	4,034	5,110	5,808	964	334
2012	3,091	4,000	5,033	6,318	1,021	241
2013	3,068	4,102	5,148	6,415	1,073	244
2014	3,095	4,217	5,329	6,856	1,097	n/d
2015	3,122	4,280	5,173	7,045	1,159	n/d
2016	2,979	n/d	5,210	7,113	1,206	n/d
2017	2,852	n/d	5,305	7,514	1,235	n/d

Source Grupo Banco Mundial (2020)

designs (after the United Kingdom; and followed by Italy, India, and China). While at the levels of competitiveness in the field of knowledge generation, it seems to maintain high ranking in the military/aerospace sector, with high added value, which generates large amounts of foreign currency from exports; but the level gets by Russia in Nobel Prize awards still doesn't match that of the Soviet Union. The Soviet Union was awarded in the fields of biology, chemistry, nuclear physics, mathematics, astronomy, achieving Nobel Prizes in these fields (1958, 1962, 1964, 1978, and in 2003 Alexei Abrikosov and Vitali Ginsburg, were awarded for their innovative work on the theory of superconductors initiated in the Soviet Union).

On the other hand, it is possible to observe that Russia ranks as 49th among 62 countries that the Human Development Index (HDI) considers to be of very high human development. It highlights an important progress from the 119th place in 2015 to the 49th place in 2016, maintaining a life expectancy of 72 years, a mortality rate of almost 13%, a per capita income of 9,508 Euros, and 12 years of average schooling according to United Nations Development Program, 2018, 2019 (Datosmacro.com, 2019).

Regarding education in Russia, which is free (although there is a private segment), what was initially observed in the first post-Soviet period is a decrease in the total number of children between 1990 and 2000, mostly pronounced in urban areas. Consequently, there was decrease in the number of children in preschool education, particularly in the years from 1990 to 1994, corresponding to the period of President Yeltsin; while this amount begins to increase at the beginning of the nineteenth century and during the period of President Putin (see Table 5.2).

Likewise, in the case of primary education, in the 1990s the number of students at this educational level was stable, decreasing in the middle of the first decade of the nineteenth century, and recovering at the beginning of the second decade. A series of factors influence this tendency, such as the aggressive incorporation of Russia into capitalism and the impacts on the society, but also the transition of the educational policy from public to private education, without proper understanding of the implication of this change (Table 5.2).

The case of secondary education is not so different from the enrollment percentage of primary education. A decrease between 1990 and 1999 was noted, which accelerates between 2004 and 2009, only to gradually recover during 2011–2017 (Table 5.2).

Therefore, despite the abrupt conditions implied by the fall of the Soviet Union, more and more children in preschool, primary and secondary education are entering formal education. This indicates the construction of a solid base with better educational conditions, although apparently affected (which is not the exception in the world), by the indiscriminate use of Communication and Information Technologies and the use of smartphones, that in excess is considered risky in shaping the intellect necessary for shaping the KBS (Kurpatov, 2020).

As mentioned above, since Adam Smith the theory gives a prominent place to the specialization of labor in production processes. Gary Baker reinterpreted this specialization in the theory of human capital, which later opens space for the endogenous economic growth theory proposed by Paul Romer.

Nowadays, aspects of a quantitative order, such as the indicators considered, are used to measure the KBE at a time when capitalism has developed to move from manufacturing to mindfacturing and, therefore, to a market for ideas that give rise to patents and intellectual authorship in the scientific and technological field.

In parallel, other approaches have focused on the development of knowledge from a social perspective, opening space for the Knowledge-Based Society, where networking has a higher transcendence.

A couple of examples of the arguments commented, particularly for Russia, show first, the opinion of scholars, government and business on science and technology, associated with education, employment, and the economy; and secondly, on the networking as the relations between individuals for specific purposes.

Regarding the first example, an approach is associated with a negative appreciation that science and technology policies are related to various areas of society, highlighting firstly, that science and technology policies are not related to the

5 The Russia's Knowledge Society

Table 5.2 HDI, pre-primary, primary, & secondary education. Russia (1990–2018)

Year	Human Development Index (HDI)[1]	Pre-primary Gross enrollment ratio (%)[2]	School enrollment, primary (% gross)[3]	School enrollment, secondary (% gross)[3]
1990	0.734 (31)	75.54	107.991	97.637
1991	0.729 (34)	74.49	110.340	96.177
1992	0.719 (40)	72.63	110.441	94.274
1993	0.711 (44)	71.71	109.481	92.078
1994	0.702 (46)	61.36	107.176	90.77
1995	0.701(118)	62.52	107.871	91.141
1996	0.702 (120)	n/a	108.483	91.475
1997	0.704 (121)	n/a	106.322	91.301
1998	0.703 (125)	n/a	103.748	92.080
1999	0.710 (123)	n/a	102.947	92.391
2000	0.721 (125)	61.36	102.791	n/a
2001	0.727 (124)	n/a	106.083	n/a
2002	0.733 (124)	n/a	113.946	n/a
2003	0.740 (125)	67.54	121.051	91.508
2004	0.746 (124)	68.27	n/a	85.316
2005	0.752 (126)	68.77	95.226	82.911
2006	0.759 (126)	70.15	94.999	82.708
2007	0.767 (126)	72.00	95.681	82.950
2008	0.774 (126)	75.84	97.585	83.127
2009	0.771 (129)	n/a	99.362	84.772
2010	0.780 (125)	75.66	n/a	n/a
2011	0.789 (124)	74.35	101.076	91.828
2012	0.797 (122)	75.81	101.021	95.607
2013	0.803 (120)	78.54	99.77	97.683
2014	0.807 (119)	82.13	97.694	98.816
2015	0.813 (119)	85.05	99.073	102.18
2016	0.817 (49)	87.13	99.814	102.397
2017	0.822 (49)	86.79	102.583	103.385
2018	0.824 (49)	n/a	n/a	n/a

Source (1) United Nation Development Programme (2019); (2) Indexmundi (2020); (3) World Bank (2020d, e)

world economic situation, followed by their dissociation from employment policies and opportunities. This is combined with a negative appreciation that science and technology are linked to educational policies, to economic structure, and to the productivity of companies (Table 5.3).

The presented data show that, from the perspective of a select group of people, there is a rupture between various state policies, that is to say that there is no or almost no relationship between the considered policies. In addition, that means that there is no comprehensive state policy oriented to the future, particularly the formation of a knowledge-based economy, centered on clear scientific-technological policies and human resources development, which could ultimately underpin the benefit expected by society as a whole.

Regarding example number two, Galán et al. (2019), highlight the close relationship of networking (Castells, 2000a, b, c; Casson, 2000; Portes, 1995); jointly to lines of communication, complexity, and chaos and self-organization (Boltansky & Chiapello, 2002), and philanthropic capitalism (Bishop & Green, 2009; Drucker, 1992) with the sanctions imposed by the West on the Eurasian country, after 2014, when a group of inter-regional and inter-personal inter-institutional networks come together to apply the sanctions imposed from abroad to Russia. Such is the case of the European Union, the US Government and organizations like the Soros Institute of Open Societies that impact the functionality of the economy, education, science, technology, altering the business environment, the training of human resources, and innovation systems within the country, affecting financial, international policy, and cybernetic aspects.

Conclusions

It is true that the process of human resources development (preschool, primary, and secondary education), in recent years has improved and is shaping a new generation that is preparing to be competitive both inside and outside the country. However, the skills development processes associated with new technologies seem to be distancing themselves from the main objective of the knowledge society that focuses on improving well-being as a whole. Some instruments implied by the KBS, in practice, may have perverse effects that distort their successful operation.

Additionally, combining the quantitative aspects with the qualitative ones, we can detect a decrease of researchers that shows the disadvantage of Russia compared to other countries located in the Northeast Asia Pacific such as Japan, South Korea, and China and others like the United States and Mexico.

Other aspect of great relevance in terms of scientific advances with application for the benefit of society is the disruption of the funding for pharmaceutical research that requires special attention (Putin, 2019). Because a large part of Russian society is used to the consumption of foreign medicines, placing the country in a high degree of dependency and risking public health security.

5 The Russia's Knowledge Society

Table 5.3 Opinion of a select group of scholars, businessmen, and government officials on Education, Science, Technology, Economic, & Social Policies relationship (2012–2014)

Question	Answer	Comments
Do you think that science and technology are currently linked to educational policies?	No, Yes, I don't know, No, No, No, No No = 5/7 = 71.4% I don't know = 1/7 = 14.3% Yes = 1/7 = 14.3%	A negative appreciation (71.4%) is overlap on science and technology being linked to educational policies
Do you think that scientific and technical policy is related to employment policy in Russia?	No, No, No, No, I don't know, No, No No = 6/7 = 85.7%, I don't know = 1/7 = 14.3%	A negative appreciation (85.7%) is superimposed on the fact that scientific and technical policy is related to employment policy
How is science and technology policy currently contributing to increased productivity in companies in Russia?	I don't know, Nothing, a little, Nothing, I don't know, I don't know, a little I don't know = 3/7 = 42.9% Nothing = 2/7 = 28.6% A Little = 2/7 = 28.6%	A negative appreciation (42.9%) is superimposed on science and technology policy contributing to the increase in productivity in companies
How are science and technology policies currently increasing employment opportunities in Russia?	Nothing, a little, a little, a little, a little, I don't know, a little Nothing = 3/7 = 42.9% A little = 3/7 = 42.9% I don't know = 1/7 = 14.3%	Overlaps that nothing or almost nothing (85.8%), science and technology policies increase employment opportunities
Do you think that science and technology policy in Russia is consistent with the economic structure?	No, Yes, I don't know, No, No, No, Yes No = 4/7 = 57.1% Yes = 2/7 = 28.6% I don't know = 1/7 = 14.3%	A negative appreciation (57.1%) is superimposed on science and technology policy being consistent with the economic structure
Do you think science and technology policy in Russia is related to job offers?	No, No, I don't know, No, No, No, No No = 6/7 = 85.7%, I don't know = 1/7 = 14.3%	A negative appreciation (85.7%) is superimposed on science and technology policy being related to job offers
Do you think that science and technology policy in Russia is related to the world economic situation?	No, No, No, No, No, No, No No = 7/7 = 100%	A negative appreciation (100%) is superimposed on science and technology policy being related to the world economic situation
Do you think that science and technology policy in Russia is related to education policy?	I don't know, Yes, I don't know, No, No, Yes, No I don't know = 2/7 = 28.6% Yes = 2/7 = 28.6% No = 3/7 = 42.9%	A negative position (42.9%) is superimposed on science and technology policy being related to education policy
Do you think that scientific and technical policy in Russia is related to the employment policy?	No, No, I don't know, No, No, No, No 6/7 = 85.7% 1/7 = 14.3%	A negative position (85.7%) is superimposed on science and technology policy being related to employment policy

(continued)

Table 5.3 (continued)

Question	Answer	Comments
Do you think that science and technology policy in Russia is related to economic policy?	No, Yes, Yes, No, No, Yes, ¿? No = 3/6 = 5.0 Yes = 3/6 = 5.0	There is no difference of opinion (50% and 50%) as to whether scientific and technological policies are related to economic policy
We appreciate you writing your comments or suggestions that will help achieve the objective of this questionnaire		There is a break between various state policies (there is no or almost no relationship, that is, there is no comprehensive state policy toward the future

Source Own elaboration based on interviews with scholars, businessmen, and government officials. Moscow, July 2012–May 2014

On the other hand, the appreciation of the select group of people from academia, business, and government, seems to confirm the distance between science and technology with other areas of the economy, politics, and society. The research shows that the incidence of science and technology is still far from the interests of society as a whole, which confirms the slowdown of post-Soviet Russia. It is still uncertain if a knowledge society of high impact can be achieved, both in the domestic sphere as well as in the competitiveness with other countries in the world. In this context, a huge task is to be carried out, especially regarding the links of scientific advances with social well-being, the main concern of a Knowledge-Based Society.

References

Becker, G. (1983). *El capital humano: un análisis teórico y empírico referido fundamentalmente a la educación*. Alianza editorial.
Bell, D. (1973). *The coming of post-industrial society*. Perseus Book Group and Basic Books.
Bishop, M., & Green, M. (2009). *Filantrocapitalismo. Cómo los ricos pueden cambiar el mundo*. Tendencias Editores.
Boltansky, L., & Chiapello, E. (2002). *El nuevo espíritu del capitalismo*. Akal.
Casson, M. (2000). *Enterprise and leadership: Studies on firms, markets and networks*. Edward Elgar.
Castells, M. (2000a). *La Era de la Información. Economía, Sociedad y Cultura* (Vol. 1, La Sociedad Red. 2 ed.). Alianza Editorial.
Castells, M. (2000b). *La Era de la Información. Economía, Sociedad y Cultura* (Vol. 2 El Poder de la Identidad. 2 ed.). Alianza Editorial.
Castells, M. (2000c). *La Era de la Información. Economía, Sociedad y Cultura* (Vol. 3 Fin de Milenio. 2 ed). Alianza Editorial.
CEPAL-UNESCO. (1992). *Educación y Conocimiento: Eje de la Transformación Productiva con Equidad*. Santiago de Chile.
Dabat-Latrubesse, A., & Rodríguez-Vargas J. D. J. (2009). *Globalización, Conocimiento y Desarrollo. La nueva economía global del conocimiento, estructura y problemas*. Tomo I.

Datosmacro.com. (2019). *Rusia-Índice de Desarrollo Humano-IDH*. https://datosmacro.expansion.com/idh/rusia.

Drucker, P. F. (1992, September–October). The new society of organizations. *Harvard Business Review*. Consultado en la página web https://hbr.org/1992/09/the-new-society-of-organizations.

Galán Amaro, E., Ricárdez Jiménez, J. D., & Rangel Delgado, J.E. (2019). *Teoría de Redes y Sanciones Económicas Impuestas a Rusia*. Seminario de Investigación sobre Rusia "Antonio Dueñas Pulido": Rusia en el Siglo XXI; Universidad Autónoma de Baja California, Marzo de 2019, Campus, Mexicali, México.

Grupo Banco Mundial. (2020). https://datos.bancomundial.org/indicador/SP.POP.SCIE.RD.P6?locations=RU-US-KR-CN-JP-MX.

https://data.worldbank.org/indicador/BX.KLT.DINV.CD.WD?locations=RU; https://data.worldbank.org/indicador/IT.NET.USER.ZS?locations=RU; https://data.worldbank.org/indicador/SE.PRM.ENRR?end=2017&locations=RU&start=1991; https://data.worldbank.org/indicador/SE.SEC.ENRR?end=2017&locations=RU&start=1990; https://www.indexmundi.com/facts/indicators/SE.PRE.ENRR/compare#country=ru.

Indexmundi. (2020). *Gross enrollment ratio*. https://www.indexmundi.com/facts/russia/school-enrollment.

Kurpatov, A. (2020). *What do expect of human digitalization?* https://www.facebook.com/100000600370843/posts/3333291786700801?sfns=m.

Machlup, F. (1962). *The production and distribution of knowledge in the United States*. Princeton University Press.

Porter, M. (1999). *La Ventaja Competitiva de las Naciones*. Vergara.

Portes, A. (1995). *The economic sociology of immigrations*: Essays on Networks, Ethnicity and entrepreneurship. Sage.

Putin, V. (2019). *Conferencia de prensa anual*. https://www.youtube.com/watch?v=idLkfLJHA1w.

Rangel Delgado, J. E., & Ivanova Boncheva, A. (2012). *The crisis in two Pacific Rim economies: Higher education and employment in Mexico and Thailand*. WTI Press.

Rangel, E., Sueyoshi, A., & Shamsiah Samsudin, R. (2018). Similarities and differences on higher education policy across the Pacific Rim: Japan, Malaysia and Mexico. *Pacific Asia Education Journal, 30*, 33–46.

Romer, P. M. (1994). The origins of endogenous growth. *The Journal of Economic Perspectives, 8*(1), 3–22.

Rossiyskaya Akademiya Nauk. (2019). *Предыстория Комиссии РАН по борьбе с лженаукой*. Е.Б. Александров, Bulletin No. 22.

Ruiz De Elvira, M. (2020). *Los científicos rusos intentan enderezar su ciencia pero la política no ayuda*. https://www.publico.es/ciencias/rusia-cientificos-rusos-enderezar-ciencia-politica-no-ayuda.html. Madrid.

Schuwab, K. (2016). *The fourth industrial revolution*. World Economic Forum.

Smith, A. (2007). *An inquiry into the nature and causes of the wealth of nations*. MetaLibri. file:///Users/erangel/Documents/SmithA_WealthNations_p.pdf.

Stiglitz, J. E., & Greenwald, B. C. (2014). *La creación de una Sociedad del Aprendizaje*. Ediciones Culturales Paidós.

Touraine (1969). *La societé post-industrielle*. Editions Denoël.

United Nation Development Programme. (2018, 2019). http://hdr.undp.org/en/data.

WIPO. (2019). *World intellectual property indicators: Filings for patents*. https://www.wipo.int/publications/en/details.jsp?id=4464Trademarks, Industrial Designs Reach Record Heights in 2018 (2019). https://www.wipo.int/pressroom/es/articles/2019/article_0012.html.

World Bank. (2020a). *Foreign direct investment, net inflows, Russian Federation*. https://data.worldbank.org/indicator/BX.KLT.DINV.WD.GD.ZS?locations=RU.

World Bank. (2020b). *Mobile cellular subscriptions (per 100 people), Russian Federation*. https://data.worldbank.org/indicator/IT.CEL.SETS.P2?locations=RU; https://data.worldbank.org/indicator/IT.CEL.SETS.P2?end=2018&locations=RU&start=1990.

World Bank. (2020c). *Individuals using the Internet (% of population)*. https://data.worldbank.org/indicator/IT.NET.USER.ZS.

World Bank. (2020d). *School enrollment, primary (% gross), Russian Federation*. https://data.worldbank.org/indicator/SE.PRM.ENRR?locations=RU.

World Bank. (2020e). *School enrollment, secondary (% gross), Russian Federation*. https://data.worldbank.org.

Chapter 6
China: Compatible Relations Between the Development of Artificial Intelligence, Employment, and Education

Aníbal Carlos Zottele Allende, Claudia Elilú Méndez Viveros, and Esteban Zottele de Vega

Abstract The scientific and technological growth presents great opportunities today, but also challenges that demand a close relationship with the economic development projects. In this aspect, the creation of higher level disciplines that train professionals in Artificial Intelligence (AI) has been encouraged. Such is the case of the investment that the People's Republic of China (PRC) has been performing in Research and Development (R&D), assigning greater importance to Information and Communication Technologies (ICTs), adapting its study plans to new global circumstances. On the other hand, in the strategy of the PRC to improve the quality of life of the population as a whole, the adaptation of AI in industrial processes is included as a central value without affecting occupation levels, although in many cases these changes affect the sign of the jobs. We conclude firstly, that until now the consequences of development have not implied massive destruction of jobs without the consequent creation of other jobs derived from the demands generated by the application of AI itself. And secondly, that opportunities related to the offers of new careers that accompany the construction of the transcendent changes in the life of humanity appear in the educational system.

Introduction

Artificial Intelligence (AI) is defined as "the capacity of a system to correctly interpret external data, to learn from this information and use it to achieve specific tasks and goals through flexible adaptation" (Kaplan & Haenlein, 2016). This type of

---

A. C. Zottele Allende (✉) · C. E. Méndez Viveros
China-Veracruz Studies Center, Veracruz University, Veracruz, Mexico
e-mail: azottele@uv.mx

C. E. Méndez Viveros
e-mail: clmendez@uv.mx

E. Zottele de Vega
Changzhou University, Changzhou, China
e-mail: ezottele@uv.mx

© The Author(s), under exclusive license to Springer Nature Singapore Pte Ltd. 2021
J. E. Rangel Delgado and A. Ivanova Boncheva (eds.), *Knowledge Society and Education in the Asia-Pacific*, SpringerBriefs in Education,
https://doi.org/10.1007/978-981-16-2333-2_6

intelligence has become relevant in recent years due to advances in science and technology (S&T) that are incorporated at high speed and that have a significant impact on world society.

This chapter shows the effect of the expansion of AI on the education sector of the People's Republic of China (PRC), favoring the creation of higher level study plans and programs that train AI professionals, especially derived from the investment that China performs in Research & Development (R&D), particularly in the field of Information and Communications Technologies ICTs.

Zhou and Zha (cited in Zottele & Zottele, 2018) affirm that: "the university is key to understanding the evolution of S&T in China" (p. 118), aspects that drive the economic and social development of the country, improving not only the quality of life of its citizens but also of the world's population.

Revolutionary advancements such as 5G and 6G connection networks, which allow connectivity on average 1000 times faster than those currently used in servers similar to Google Fiber—one of the fastest in the data transfer market—, are a clear example of what China intends to achieve. That is why it prepares its workforce, which will provide benefits not only in industrial and economic sectors, but also in the environment, since these new technologies will favor different aspects related to the quality of the environment, including positive advances to mitigate the climate change.

China is an important global protagonist in AI, in some cases surpassing the United States in areas previously dominated by this country, because of measures implemented by the eastern country to foster its technological capacity and causing a unique articulation with the use of these advances by its population.

This is manifested in the rapid transformation of the daily social life and of broad sectors of industry, commerce, medicine, and security, sparked by the incorporation of AI. Reason that has given rise to reaffirm the need to create original systems of training of skilled labor for the management of these new technologies. Some of these AI-induced processes in people's daily lives are considered in this chapter, particularly with the aforementioned generation of new and better jobs for society not only in China, but globally.

China's Place in AI Development

The evolution of AI has generated benefits for humanity and for the environment. It has become a major issue for nations, particularly the United States and China, which invest large resources that represent a growing proportion of their GDP.

The current interest has been recognized since the emergence of the concept of Artificial Intelligence, first proposed in 1956 by John McCarthy, Marvin Minsky, and Claude Shannon. Its importance and relevance for the socioeconomic growth of the countries were established before the origin of the aforementioned concept, but it especially accompanied the prestige acquired by another one of the great inventions of the twentieth century: The Internet.

For the PRC, the development of science and technology (S&T) has played a major role in its economic growth. Lin (2019), points out that technological innovation is the answer for any country in search of development. However, during the Industrial Revolution its epicenter was located in Western Europe. China and other countries in Asia, Latin America, and Africa did not have a significant role in it. At that time, these regions became the periphery of the rapidly industrializing European countries.

In particular, China, ruled at that time by the Qing Dynasty, suffered the Opium Wars (first from 1839 to 1842 and after from 1856 to 1860) led by Great Britain. The greatest western power of that time managed to impose conditions derived from its military power, extending its predominance not only throughout the nineteenth century but also during most of the twentieth century.

With the growth of the PRC, great transformations were generated that included the literacy of all young people and increasingly the adult population, the inclusion of women who until then were outside the productive system, and also the consolidation of the bases of autonomous S&T development.

In 1978, with the beginning of the modernization process, Deng Xiaoping adopted an approach where economic opening, changes in agricultural and industrial production and marketing systems, allowed the accelerated GDP growth. Starting in the 1990s, the presence of foreign investment became active, positioning S&T as one of the central topics.

Since then, China has given decisive importance to this factor in order to achieve sustained growth. For this reason, the government, the private sector, and the academy have worked together to create the ideal environment for the generation of an AI ecosystem, which guarantees its important role at the international level.

Under this context, in July 2017 the government published The New Generation Artificial Intelligence Development Plan, which aims to increase the value of the industry. In the same year, the Chinese Minister of Science and Technology, Wan Gang, pointed out "national investment in R&D amounted to around 1.76 trillion yuan (269.6 billion dollars), that is, 70.9 percent more than in 2012." This level of public spending has been increasing until it exceeded the figures for financing for this item with respect to actors such as the sum of the member countries of the European Union, putting the nation on the path to becoming an AI leader by 2030 (Zottele & Zottele, 2018) (Table 6.1).

China has promoted research and development work on AI, ranking first as the nation that publishes the most articles, according to data from the "AI Index Report 2019" (Perrault, 2019), demonstrating the great interest that society has in the evolution through science. In addition, the commitment that the Chinese government has to achieve these objectives, has been distinguished as one of the main strengths of this nation, since its participation and guidance have formed a top-down enabling environment that provides confidence to investors and intellectuals to collaborate and contribute to the cause.

The PRC has another great quality that makes its potential in this field more dynamic and consists of a large number of Internet users on its territory; providing an extraordinary accumulation of information and data that no other nation has, obtaining the necessary know-how to create more and better technology.

Table 6.1 Recent AI plans

Plan	Description	Key elements	Importance
13th Five-Year Plan for the Developing of National and Emerging Industries (2016–2020)	A State Council policy document which specifies implementation measures for the 13th Five-Year Plan, focused on strategic industries	Highlighted development of AI as 6th among 69 major tasks for the central government to pursue; identified five agencies responsible for developing central government policies in AI in the next five years	Links AI to the current Five-Year Plan through this guiding plan
"Internet Plus" and AI Three-Year Implementation Plan (2016–2018)	Jointly issued by the National Development and Reform Commission (NDRC), the Ministry of Science and Technology (MoST), Ministry of Industry and Information (MIIT), and the Cyberspace Administration of China	Established a goal to grow the scale of the AI industry's market size to the "hundreds of billions" (RMB)	Connects AI development to highly touted "Internet Plus" policy which aims to catapult China to becoming a digital powerhouse
Robotics Industry Development Plan (2016–2020)	Plan to develop robotics industry released by the NDRC, the MIIT, and the Ministry of Finance (MOF)	Set specific targets for advancing the robotics industry, the second of two development plans containing a focus on AI released by central agencies with a policy planning mandate	Sets goal of manufacturing 100,000 industrial robots annually by 2020, making China the world's leading robot-maker
"Artificial Intelligence 2.0"	Proposal by Chinese Academy of Engineering added to a list of 15 "SciTech Innovation 2030-Megaprojects"	Megaprojects were proposed and finalized in 2016 with the release of the "13th Five Year Plan for National Science and Technology Innovation" but AI was added in February 2017	Demonstrates how AI was elevated to the level of a megaproject only recently

(continued)

Table 6.1 (continued)

Plan	Description	Key elements	Importance
Three-Year Action Plan for Promoting Development of a New Generation Artificial Intelligence Industry (2018–2020)	MIIT action plan for implementing tasks related to State Council's AI Plan and "Made in China 2025"	Sets out specific benchmarks for 2020 in a range of AI products and services, including smart, internet-connected cars, and intelligent service robots	Shows government's strong guiding role in developing the AI industry (convened top 30 companies to develop indicators)

Source Own elaboration with data obtained from Faggella (2019)

Until now, the creation of the 5G network and the development of 6G gives the People's Republic of China a privileged place as power and advantages in various areas such as logistics, telemedicine, virtual reality, data transfer, security, communications, etc. This allows attracting not only Foreign Direct Investment (FDI), but also talents from different origins around the world.

All of this has favored the strategy of "sub-national China," since each of the provinces is facing, according to its interests, needs, and possibilities, these national objectives, implementing its own public policies related to the emergence of technology development companies and training of labor for these.

Cities such as the country's capital Beijing and Tianjin, an important port in northeast China, have given greater weight to the education sector as a catalyst for the synergistic trio between AI research, production, and development, holding important events that bring together specialists from around the world, as well as the construction of focused and dedicated industrial parks.

In this way, the PRC has recognized the importance that education has in creating and attracting new minds that contribute to the scope of the Chinese technological dream. It is important to consider that there are other factors besides investment, which allow strengthening the competitive advantage of a country in terms of AI. Thus, more and more universities offer careers geared toward technological development, also fostered by the demand for specialists in the area, due to the increase in the number of employers in this sector and immigration policies more open to attract geniuses in this branch of science.

Adaptation of Education to New Global Circumstances and Challenges

PriceWaterhouseCoopers published a study carried out in 2017, which shows the impact that the adoption of AI will have worldwide, and estimates that global GDP will increase by 14% by 2030. There are three main reasons for this increasing: modifications to productivity gains because of process automation, productivity increases due to the empowerment of the workforce, and consumption thanks to the accessibility of more specialized, higher quality, and personalized products (Table 6.2).

In the same way, this disruptive process is causing changes in the educational sector. Because of these new global circumstances of growth and development and the innovative features of current populations, educational institutions are forced to train other types of professionals capable of assuming new and different skills; integrating knowledge societies that seek learning by the use of information for the creation and management of instruments that incorporate AI.

In this sense, China has identified the opportunities and challenges that arise in this adaptation phase, since not only does AI require these modifications, but also other aspects such as S&T, Big Data, or Blockchain, which need versatile individuals capable of adjusting quickly to the constant technological evolution.

Thus, China's training system, mainly in its higher education, aims to forge learning through the combination of multiple disciplines, where people are able to operate, program, and work with large-scale software and hardware, applicable in both fields, business and social. This must be performed without violating human and ecological rights due to bad practices or applications, which is why it is intended that the so-called "new generation of AI" learn to coexist with the emerging technologies, managing themselves through a strict adherence to ethics.

In 2019, the New Generation AI Committee of Experts on Governance published the principles through which people with the highest IQ will be educated in the responsible development of AI in the country, which include: harmony and friendship; equity and justice; inclusion and exchange; respect for privacy; security and control capacity; shared responsibility; open cooperation and agile management.

Therefore, China stands out as a responsible country in the development and management of AI, making it safe, controllable, and reliable for the world population, largely responding to international questions about its use in the field of security. The contribution is not only for the PRC, since in the fight against climate change AI is considered as an indisputable ally to help the planet.

Emergence of New Careers Related to Artificial Intelligence

Meanwhile, this growing demand for talent has led the Chinese government to establish educational programs within its universities, aimed at training and preparing people in the area of AI, transforming its institutions into the fundamental force to build a prosperous technology industry.

China currently leads the ranking of the countries that carry out the most scientific publications on AI, even ahead of the United States—its main competitor. However, their impact is not as expected, since in this area it is still below the first positions. Working on the quality of R&D generated in the nation is essential intending to be the world technological leader (Table 6.3).

6 China: Compatible Relations Between the Development … 71

Table 6.2 Index of potential impact of artificial intelligence on consumption

Sector	Subsector	Potential AI consumption impact	Personalization	Time saved	Utility	Data reliability
Healthcare		3.7	3.8	2.7	3.9	4.4
	Providers/health services	3.9	4.1	3.0	3.9	4.7
	Pharma/life sciences	3.8	3.9	2.8	4.2	7.1
	Insurance	3.6	3.6	2.6	3.8	4.2
	Consumer health	3.5	3.4	2.3	3.4	4.8
Automotive		3.7	3.9	2.9	3.8	3.9
	Aftermarket % repair	3.9	4.2	2.8	3.6	4.6
	Component suppliers	3.9	4.0	2.0	3.5	5.0
	Personal mobility as a service	3.8	4.0	3.7	4.0	3.7
	OEM	3.6	4.0	3.0	4.0	3.5
	Financing	3.3	3.3	3.0	3.7	3.0
Financial services		3.3	2.8	2.6	3.2	4.6
	Asset wealth management	3.4	2.9	2.2	3.7	4.3
	Banking and capital	3.3	2.5	2.9	3.0	5.0
	Insurance	3.2	3.1	2.4	3.1	4.4
Transportation and logistics		3.2	3.5	2.6	3.3	3.7
	Transportation	3.5	3.0	2.8	3.5	5.0
	Logistics	3.1	3.9	2.5	3.1	3.0
Technology, communications and entertainment		3.1	2.5	2.1	3.3	4.3
	Technology	3.3	2.7	2.4	3.6	4.1
	Entertainment, media and communication	3.0	2.5	2.0	3.3	4.4
Retail		3.0	2.8	2.1	3.3	3.8
	Consumer products	3.1	3.0	2.3	3.3	3.8
	Retail	3.0	2.6	2.0	3.3	3.7
Energy		2.2	3.2	2.1	3.1	3.1

(continued)

Table 6.2 (continued)

Sector	Subsector	Potential AI consumption impact	Personalization	Time saved	Utility	Data reliability
	Oil & gas	2.3	4.0	2.1	2.9	3.0
	Power & utilities	2.1	2.0	2.1	3.3	3.2
Manufacturing		2.2	2.0	1.2	3.7	3.8
	Industrial manufacturing	2.2	2.0	1.4	3.7	3.9
	Industrial products/raw materials	2.1	N/A	1.0	3.6	3.7

Source Own elaboration with data obtained from PriceWaterhouseCoopers (2017)

Table 6.3 Institutions that lead in quality R&D in AI

Institution	Country/region	Publications	Field-weighted citation impact
Massachusetts Institute of Technology	United States	1011	3.57
Carnegie Mellon University	United States	1311	2.53
Nanyang Technological University	Singapore	1197	2.51
University of Granada	Spain	587	2.46
University of Southern California	United States	627	2.35
Technical University of Munich	Germany	656	2.27
Institute of Automation, Chinese Academy of Sciences	China	588	2.26
Hong Kong Polytechnic University	Hong Kong	602	2.20
National University of Singapore	Singapore	807	2.14
Chinese University of Hong Kong	Hong Kong	530	2.09

Source Times Higher Education. Consulted December 2019. https://www.timeshighereducation.com/data-bites/which-countries-and-universities-are-leading-ai-research

6 China: Compatible Relations Between the Development … 73

Table 6.4 Syllabus of the first semester of bachelor's degree from Nanjing University School in IA

Serial number	Course number	Name of the course	Credits	Hours
1	30000110	Data Structure and Algorithm Analysis	4.4	4.4
2	30000100	Probability and Mathematical Statistics	4.4	4.4
3	30000120	Optimization Method	2	2
4.4	30000130	Computer system base	5.5	5.5
5.5	30000040	Introduction to artificial intelligence	2	2
6.6	00000010	Introduction to the basic principles of Marxism	3	3
7.7	00000080C	Situation and politics	1	1
8	00040010C	Physical Education (3)	1	2
9.9	30000360	Introduction to neuroscience	2	2
10	30000140	Introduction to databases	2	2
11	30000380	Smart hardware and new devices	2	2
12	30000410	Smart application modeling	2	2

Source Nanjing University Official Site. https://ai.nju.edu.cn/8e/98/c18529a429720/page.htm

Each one of the universities of China is attracting national and international students offering degrees aimed at the development of S&T. The most recent example is Nanjing University, which has degrees in Machine Learning and Data Mining, and Intelligent Systems and Applications, whose study plans are perfected through practical learning, since the entity's alliance with the company Jingdong (JD) in particular, will provide students with real data on electronic commerce, logistics, and finance, enhancing their ability to create truly useful cutting-edge technology (Table 6.4).

The relative growth of international schools that provided data for the years 2010–2019 is shown in Chart 6.1. Here the University of Toronto (Canada) has the highest number of students registered for Introduction to IA + ML, followed by the School of Economy (Russia) and Tsinghua University (China) in 2018.

On the other hand, compared to 2015, enrollment has grown to four times its size at Tsinghua University, three times at the University of Toronto, and twice at the University of Melbourne (Chart 6.2).

Jobs Generated from AI Development and Non-replacement of Labor

The widespread fear of AI—which is quickly suggested with the image of a robot—, has led us to believe that its incorporation into the productive life of companies will lead to the massive dismissal and increase of poverty rates worldwide, marking even more the class difference.

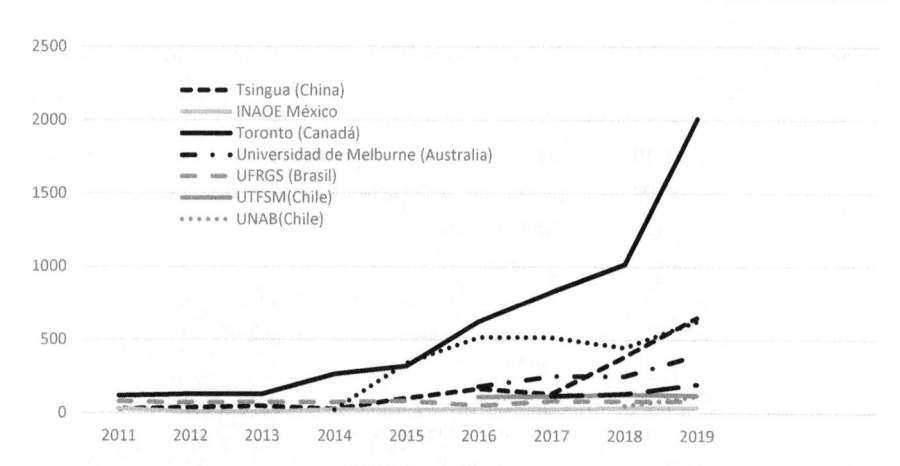

Chart 6.1 Enrollment in AI and ML courses. *Source* Own elaboration with data obtained from Perrault (2019)

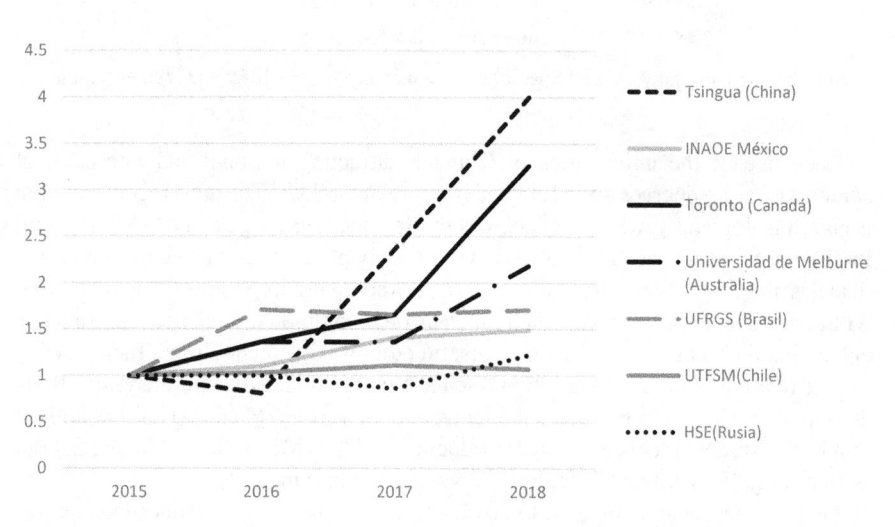

Chart 6.2 Growth in enrollment in IA and ML programs with reference to 2015. *Source* Own elaboration with data obtained from Perrault (2019)

What is not common knowledge is that today giant AI-based platforms already operate in the labor market: the bank credit system is the largest example of this fact, practically all members of civil society are evaluated by intelligent software that determines, for example, our credit quality and they decide based on it to grant or not a loan.

For this reason, the idea of substituting machines for men should not be taken as an evil per se, since the development of AI has a positive impact on people's lives, even on their daily work, according to the characteristics and priorities of the economic system and according to the policies in which AI is implemented. Although the

Technological Revolution, like the Industrial Revolution, implied a paradigm shift, this time the transition has other characteristics and, in principle, the generation of jobs does not have the negative implications of other transformations.

Even though unemployment is a probability in this phase of readjustment to new ways of doing things, AI countries, like China, are planning to replace the positions that will be automated (carried out by a machine), through the emergence of new activities that a robot cannot perform.

Creativity and communication are examples of the deficiencies that machines or robots show, representing potential opportunities, since the generation of greater benefit should be expressed in better working conditions and remuneration.

In this context, China is also promoting other study degrees that, in addition to those specifically related to AI, rather than having to do with the exact sciences such as mathematics, statistical computing, etc., are oriented to social relationships such as psychology, non-verbal language, philosophy, pedagogy, etc., opening even more the range of possibilities to be used.

Applications of the Chinese Experience in Mexico

Big changes produce big challenges, therefore a wide variety of solutions. Education is the main universal response to any type of challenge and the PRC has made it the main ally for its development.

China is betting on sustained growth through the generation of AI, by establishing a strong base in education, which will improve the quality of its future workforce and therefore its economy. Thus, the country is dedicating extensive resources, efforts, and time to the training of its population, a measure that will bring great results in the not too distant future.

As a country that is among the world's principal economies, so is its educational level, and that allows it to make pertinent decisions to the role that the nation plays in the global context.

For Mexico, and in general for Latin American countries, it is imperative to generate higher level careers and programs that instruct new generations in the creation and management of new technologies, following the example of the People's Republic of China, since It depends on them to be competitive in the game of globalization. Although there is significant progress, the initiatives that some public and private academic institutions have assumed must still be generalized.

In a study published and developed by Latinoamérica (2019), in which Mexico's current position regarding AI adoption is presented, it is highlighted that:

In a simulation of maximum adoption of Artificial Intelligence technology in the next 10 years, Mexico could increase its GDP growth rate from current projections of 2.4% annual average growth until 2030, to levels ranging from 4.6 to 6.4%. This boost could be accompanied by an increase in productivity and demand for more skilled workers. Under this scheme, the business services industry would be the most benefited, with 9.4 million new jobs or the equivalent of new working hours (109% of additional jobs in 2030).

In terms of professions, highly skilled positions could increase by 67% for the next decade. In six of the seven largest sectors that were analyzed (Public Sector, Business Services, Commerce, Hospitality and Tourism, Construction, Manufacturing, Mining, Agriculture and Public Services), the demand for highly qualified jobs is expected to increase. Service businesses would require 8.9 million additional highly skilled workers (221% more jobs or the equivalent in working hours); manufacturing, 1.8 million (92%); and construction, 1 million (157%).

However and even when Mexico is in a position to accelerate the adoption of AI, the aforementioned weaknesses that still underlie—despite the also indicated progress—in the education system may leave out the benefits of this process and of the new market a large part of the Mexican population. For this reason, the difficulties in accessing higher education and new technologies do not guarantee correct assimilation of these new AI proposals.

Although the country has the possibility of having an active participation in the global environment of AI, its educational backwardness is one of the limits to the full use of this opportunity. For this reason, the Chinese experience shows the need for an accelerated restructuring of curricula and programs, especially at the tertiary level, which especially incorporate not only the specific aspects of innovations but also their social implications, including in them aspects related to the academic training of new generations.

Conclusions

After a millennial history in which China was a central country in manufacturing and trade, it became a peripheral nation with a minimal economic impact at the global level, with the predominance of the economies of Western Europe and the United States in the late nineteenth century and much of the twentieth century. However, it has once again become one of the leading nations of the twenty-first century.

Especially after the crisis of the developed western economies in 2008–2009, and after a sustained growth of more than 30 years, the anti-cyclical policies that it developed placed it in the center of the world scene and today it has become one of the main references in all the activities of the global society.

In this process, the purpose of generating an autonomous S&T development that comes from the origin of the creation of the PRC, acquired a primary role.

With the modernization, process that began in 1978 with the leadership of Deng Xiaoping, China opened up to the world and 15 years later it began to perform through FDI on a large scale, a new technological leap. The presence of thousands of multinational companies contributed to turn the country into the recipient of the world's industrial activity.

In addition to this, a flexible and inclusive educational process awakened the intellectual potential of a society with a great tradition of innovations recognized by the world since the first centuries of the Christian era. Therefore, it is not surprising that this history and the profound changes of recent decades make it one of the leading countries in the generation and application of AI.

This leadership has as main support two factors that give confidence to the members of Chinese society. The first is that until now the consequences of development have not implied a massive destruction of jobs without the consequent creation of other jobs derived from the demands generated by the application of AI itself. The second is that opportunities related to the offers of new careers that accompany the construction of these transcendent changes in the life of humanity appear in the educational system.

The Chinese experience in this specific aspect is extremely useful to establish some mechanism for creative updating of the educational process in Mexico, within a dynamic transformation process like the one performed in many Chinese universities.

References

Faggella, D. (2019). AI in China—Recent history, strengths and weaknesses of the ecosystem. *EMERJ*. https://emerj.com/ai-market-research/ai-in-china-recent-history-strengths-and-weaknesses-of-the-ecosystem/.

Kaplan, A., & Haenlein, M. (2016). Higher education and the digital revolution: About MOOCs, SPOCs, social media, and the Cookie Monster. *Business Horizons* (pp. 441–450). Elsevier.

Latinoamérica, N. C. (2019). Impulsado por Inteligencia Artificial, México podría cuadriplicar el aumento en la productividad laboral e incrementar su PIB hasta un 6.4%. *News Center Microsoft Latinoamericana*. https://news.microsoft.com/es-xl/impulsado-por-inteligencia-artificial-mexico-podria-cuadriplicar-el-aumento-en-la-productividad-laboral-e-incrementar-su-pib-hasta-un-6-4/.

Lin, J. Y. (2019). Demystifying the Chinese economy. Cambridge University Press.

Perrault, R. (2019). *Artificial intelligence index report 2019*. Stanford Human-Centered Artificial Intelligence HAI. https://hai.stanford.edu/sites/default/files/ai_index_2019_report.pdf.

PriceWaterhouseCoopers España. (2017). La Inteligencia Artificial impulsará el PIB mundial un 14% en 2030 por sus efectos en la productividad y en el consumo. *PriceWaterhouseCoopers España*. https://www.pwc.es/es/sala-prensa/notas-prensa/2017/la-inteligencia-artificial-impulsara-pib-mundial.html.

Zottele, A., & Zottele, E. (2018). Políticas de educación, ciencia y tecnología en China: innovación al servicio del desarrollo económico. In A. Ivanova, L. Morales & R. Ernesto (Eds.), *Ciencia, Tecnología e Innovación para el desarrollo. Baja California Sur* (pp. 113–126). Guidelines.

Chapter 7
Higher Education, Knowledge Economy, and Tourism Competitiveness in the APEC Area

Carlos Mario Amaya Molinar, Juan Carlos Yáñez Velazco, and Irma Magaña Carrillo

Abstract The chapter explores the relationship between tourism activity and the knowledge-based economy. To this purpose, a case study of the economies affiliated to the Asia-Pacific cooperation mechanism is examined. Documentary research techniques are applied on academic literature, institutional documents, and databases. Concepts on knowledge society and economy, tourism epistemology and system are reviewed. Indicators on knowledge management and competitiveness are consulted; as well as databases on the knowledge economy, investment in research and development, human capital, higher education coverage, and international travel statistics. The final part of the document analyzes the cases of three institutions of tertiary education dedicated to the superior academic training of qualified personnel for tourism industry. The findings include a relationship between investment in research, tourism competitiveness, and utilization of attractions, as well as some resistance of tourist organizations to adopt knowledge management systems.

Introduction

This chapter studies the relationship between knowledge economy and tourism in the economies of the Asia-Pacific Economic Cooperation (APEC). The work consists of two parts: firstly, we present a review of academic literature on the knowledge economy, and, secondly, we analyze the tourism in the APEC region in relation to the knowledge economy, tourism competitiveness, and the superior academic training of tourism professionals. In this context, we contrast the concepts of knowledge

C. M. Amaya Molinar (✉) · I. Magaña Carrillo
School of Tourism, University of Colima, Colima, Mexico
e-mail: carlos_amaya@ucol.mx

I. Magaña Carrillo
e-mail: irma@ucol.mx

J. C. Yáñez Velazco
School of Pedagogy, University of Colima, Colima, Mexico
e-mail: jcyanez@ucol.mx

© The Author(s), under exclusive license to Springer Nature Singapore Pte Ltd. 2021
J. E. Rangel Delgado and A. Ivanova Boncheva (eds.), *Knowledge Society and Education in the Asia-Pacific*, SpringerBriefs in Education,
https://doi.org/10.1007/978-981-16-2333-2_7

society and knowledge economy, highlighting that the knowledge economy presents a more concrete and tangible approach, and the knowledge societies approach is more idealistic and aspirational. As an economic cooperation body, APEC's approach is oriented more to economies rather than countries or cultures. The first section reviews different approaches, methodologies, and some results developed by the World Bank related to the knowledge economy. It also includes a review of the indicators for measuring competitiveness used by the World Economic Forum.

The second part analyzes the tourism in the APEC economies in the light of the knowledge economy, the indicators for measuring the tourism competitiveness of the World Economic Forum and the information provided by the World Tourism Organization. We provide the description of tourism, and the advances in the epistemological conception of tourism, and some limitations and challenges faced by actors and researchers of the tourism industry regarding knowledge management. Finally, we review the educational practices of three universities dedicated to train tourism professionals. The findings based on the review of academic literature, institutional documents, and databases show a relationship between investment in research and development, higher education, and human capital formation with tourism competitiveness and the use of tourism resources.

The Knowledge Industry

Although Drucker (1969) did not introduce the concept "knowledge economy," he contributed more to its dissemination, because of his great influence among academicians and managers. Drucker highlighted that the knowledge industries increased their share in the US gross domestic product (GDP) from 25% in 1955 to one-third in 1965 and predicted an increase to 50% in the 1970s. Drucker defines the knowledge industries as those that do not distribute products and services, but ideas and information. Therefore, 90% of all scientists and technologists who existed in the history of humanity are alive and in operation, represented by all those knowledge workers who apply ideas, concepts, and information instead of manual or physical skills.

Drucker's approaches (1969) to the role of knowledge in the economy are based on the work of Machlup (1962), who defines knowledge production as an economic activity or industry. In contrast to agriculture, mining, industries of steel and paper, and retail trade, that have been profoundly studied, knowledge production remained an area of activity neglected by economic science, even though the relationship between knowledge-generating work versus physical work is strongly associated with increases in productivity and the rate of economic growth. We can distinguish four types of knowledge: practice (professional, business, labor, political, domestic, etc.), intellectual, colloquial-recreational, and spiritual. Alike any industry, the production of knowledge requires substantial investments and specific staff, normally university professors who develop research in higher education institutions together with the students.

Table 7.1 Fields of economic activity that are part of the knowledge economy

Economic sectors	Areas of activity
EDUCATION	Basic, medium, high school, postgraduate
RESEARCH AND DEVELOPMENT	Basic and applied research, innovation, invention, discovery, patents, relationships with industry and higher education
SOCIAL MEDIA	Press, photography, audio, theater, cinema, radio, TV, advertising and public relations, telephone, telegraph, mail, conferences
COMPUTERS	Information devices Measurement, observation, and control mechanisms. Electronic computers
INFORMATION SERVICES	Knowledge industries Professional knowledge services: legal services, engineering and architecture, accounting, medical services
FINANCIAL INFORMATION SERVICES	Banks, stockbrokers, insurers, real estate
WHOLESALE	Wholesale merchants

Source Machlup (1962)

The forerunner on the knowledge economy is the book entitled The Production and Distribution of Knowledge in the United States (Machlup, 1962), where the fields of activity characteristic of the knowledge economy are presented (Table 7.1). In addition to the areas of education, research, and development, the field called "Computer Machines" is introduced. This was incipient at the time of publication of the work, but with exponential growth since the 80 s, and performing a significant multiplier effect on the rest of the areas included. Similarly, the social media sector has developed substantially, together with the tourism activity, in response to the increased workers' free time, derived from the introduction of a 40-hour working week.

Society and Knowledge Economy

Analyzing the differences between knowledge society and knowledge economy, Sörlin and Vessuri (2007) define the economy as an integral part of society, concluding that the knowledge society is an ideal situation, utopian to some extent, which is expected to be reached in an imprecise future, while the knowledge economy is very real and concrete, based on the logic of production and market, and associated with power. The knowledge society develops alongside the mass university education initiated at the end of World War II, and to be consolidated, a large proportion of the population must have university studies.

In the 1950s, Mincer (1958) introduced the concept of human capital, while Solow (1956) analyzed the role of technology in the economy, demonstrating the important role of both factors in increasing the productivity of the industrialized countries. Later, Bell (1973) formulates the theory of post-industrial society, characterized by high productivity, high-income population, and migration of workers to the tertiary sector, moving away from extractive and industrial activities. Similarly, at this new stage, the population tends to allocate ever-increasing parts of their income to non-basic goods and services, such as health, specialized services, entertainment, art, and travel, among others, which in turn generates an increasing demand for academically qualified personnel to provide such services.

Knowledge-based economies showed substantially higher rates and volumes of growth than the rest of the world's countries, positioning universities as central prerequisites to participate in this new stage of capitalism, with university graduates earning ever-increasing incomes, far superior to workers without such training. Thus, the knowledge society generated a more divided and unequal society, between university graduates and those who are not. In addition, the authors point out that, at the beginning of the twenty-first century, the increase in universities, university graduates, the expansion of the knowledge economy, and investment in research and development have been concentrated in a few countries, specifically the members the Organization for Cooperation and Development (OECD), concentrating 80% of the global funds allocated to these concepts (Sörlin & Vessuri, 2007). Although some developing countries exponentially increased financial resources for these items, the gap with advanced economies remains, with the countries of North America and Western Europe as leaders, concentrating the 500 most prestigious universities in the world.

Clearly, knowledge management leads to a close correlation between science, technology, and power, especially when most funds are considered to be oriented to applied research, leaving the basic sciences behind. The primacy of the knowledge economy over the knowledge society has generated criticism from various authors. The knowledge society suggests widespread education, accessible information technologies for the entire population, and new cultural communities based on the dissemination of information. However, nowadays knowledge is regarded as capital, assuming the economic meaning of the term, without considering the democratic or ethical dimensions of science and scientific institutions (Castelfranchi, 2007). In the same context, global political discourse considers knowledge important for its instrumental or commercial usefulness, relegating research on topics such as culture, the arts, the humanities, and the social sciences. Rooney and Ninan (2005) criticize the technocratic guidance generated by knowledge management systems, developed mainly in the field of information technologies.

Knowledge Management

Despite the disappointment shown by some academicians about the commercialization and industrial or utilitarian use of knowledge, international institutions such as the World Bank (2007) strongly support policies aimed at fostering the knowledge economy in the least advanced countries, considering it a basis for development. The World Bank presents as example the cases of Finland, Ireland, and South Korea, countries that during the second half of the twentieth century implemented policies aimed at boosting the knowledge economy, obtaining positive results in relatively short timeframes. In addition to overcoming ancestral lags, they managed to rank among the most competitive countries in the world, generating considerable advances in their levels of socioeconomic development. Based on these premises, this international financial institution proposed the program called Knowledge for Development (K4D) supported by four pillars (Table 7.2).

The World Bank developed the Knowledge Assessment Methodology (KAM), publishing online tools that allowed the interested public to evaluate a set of socioeconomic indicators of countries to generate the Knowledge Economy Index (World Bank, 2007). Various versions of this methodology have been presented; a basic

Table 7.2 The 4 pillars of the knowledge for development program

Pillar 1	Pillar 2	Pillar 3	Pillar 4
Economic and institutional regime	Education and skills	Information and communication infrastructure	Innovation system
Public policies aimed at boosting the use and acquisition of new knowledge for economic activity, the improvement of quality and promoting innovation and creation of new companies	Promote education and population development to create, share, and make better use of knowledge	Integrate infrastructures that facilitate effective communication, dissemination, and processing of information	The country's innovation system, made up of companies, research centers, universities, consultants, and think tanks, requires developing the capacity to leverage the growing acquis of global knowledge, assimilating and integrating it into creating new technologies that drive the development of new products and competitive processes in the international market and meeting local needs

Source World Bank (2007)

Table 7.3 Basic variables of the knowledge assessment methodology

Performance (2)	Economic incentives and institutional regimes (3)	Education and human resources (3)	Innovation system (7)	Information infrastructure (3)
• GDP growth (percentage) • Human Development Index	• Tariff and non-tariff barriers • Regulatory quality • States of Law	• Adult literacy rate • Secondary enrollment • Tertiary enrollment	• Spending on R&D • R&D researchers, people per million • Patents granted by the country • Patent application • Patents granted to residents. • Payments and royalties for use of intellectual property • Scientific and technological articles, people per million	• Phones per thousand people • Computers per thousand people • Internet users per thousand people

Source World Bank (2007)

version includes six variables and a set of indicators exposed in Table 7.3. The work on that same methodology of Chen and Dahlman (2005) analyzes a total of 80 variables, proposing a basic control board with 14 standard variables: two performance and: 12 knowledge, with three variables representing each of the four pillars of the knowledge economy, with the possibility of formulating appropriate measurements to the needs of users.

Statistics from the United Nations Educational, Scientific and Cultural Organization (UNESCO) show that, during 2017, the world invested 1.7% of GDP in research and development, with varying levels of contribution between countries and actors. The regions of the world with most investment in this area are the United States and Western Europe (2.5%), Asia and the Pacific (2.1%); and with the lowest levels, Central Asia (0.2), Arab countries (0.5), and Sub-Saharan Africa (0.4). For their part, Latin American and Caribbean countries invest an average of 0.7% of their GDP. The five countries in the world that invest the most in research and development are, in that order, the United States of America, China, Japan, Germany, and South Korea (UNESCO, 2018).

With regard to sources of funding, it is important to note that most of the investment in development research globally, and especially in those countries that invest the most in research and development, comes from private companies, followed by

7 Higher Education, Knowledge Economy ...

governments, universities, and private non-profit organizations. Thus, most of the investment comes from private sources, with majority of these resources oriented toward business purposes. Private companies and governments often work with universities to develop research projects. Table 7.4 presents the share of GDP that the economies of the Asia-Pacific Cooperation Mechanism (APEC) invested in research and development during 2018. In the field of information and communication technologies, it is worth to mention that, currently, among the 10 companies with the highest market capitalization in the world, seven are technological (Statista, 2020).

The measurement of the Knowledge Economy Index at the Asia-Pacific Economic Cooperation (APEC) Forum yields the results shown in Table 7.5. Stands out the advanced position of OECD, English-speaking, and commonwealth countries; among the Ibero-American countries, only Chile is located at the top of the table. The measurement was performed using the World Bank Institute's Knowledge Assessment Methodology (KAM).

For some unknown reason, the World Bank suspended publications on the knowledge economy index in 2012, although not the European Bank for Reconstruction

Table 7.4 Investment in research and development by APEC countries

No.	Country	% GDP
1	South Korea	4.3
2	Japan	3.4
3	United States	2.7
4	Australia	2.2
5	Singapore	2.1
6	China	2
7	Canada	1.7
8	Malaysia	1.3
9	New Zealand	1.2
10	Russia	1.1
11	Hong Kong	0.7
12	Mexico	0.5
13	Thailand	0.4
14	Viet Nam	0.4
15	Chile	0.4
16	Indonesia	0.1
17	Philippines	0.1
18	Peru	0.1
19	Brunei	0
20	Papua New Guinea	Nd
21	Taiwan	Nd

Source UNESCO (2018)

Table 7.5 Index and range in the knowledge economy among the countries of the Asia-Pacific Economic Cooperation (APEC)

N°	Country	Knowledge economy index	Knowledge index	Economic incentives regime	Innovation	Education	ICTs	2008 range
1	Canada	9.21	9.14	9.42	9.43	9.26	8.74	6
2	United States	9.08	9.05	9.16	9.45	8.77	8.93	9
3	Australia	9.05	9.17	8.66	8.72	9.64	9.16	10
4	New Zealand	8.87	9	8.48	8.65	9.79	8.56	15
5	Taiwan	8.69	8.8	8.35	9.24	7.91	9.26	17
6	Japan	8.56	8.84	7.71	9.15	8.71	8.66	19
7	Singapore	8.24	7.75	9.71	9.56	5.19	8.5	24
8	Hong Kong	8.2	7.73	9.6	8.64	5.3	9.26	26
9	South Korea	7.68	8.38	5.57	8.47	7.97	8.71	31
10	Chile	6.92	6.53	8.11	6.81	6.31	6.46	40
11	Malaysia	6.06	6.02	6.18	6.83	4.14	7.08	48
12	Russian Federation	5.4	6.69	1.55	6.89	7.09	6.08	49
13	Mexico	5.45	5.48	5.38	5.82	4.85	5.77	60
14	Thailand	5.44	5.41	5.51	5.98	5.27	5	61
15	Peru	4.64	4.86	3.98	3.88	5.57	5.12	74
16	China	4.35	4.46	4.01	5.12	4.11	4.16	77
17	Philippines	4.25	4.02	4.95	3.63	4.76	3.66	79
18	Indonesia	3.23	3.19	3.36	3.32	3.42	2.82	98
19	Vietnam	3.02	3.08	2.85	2.83	3.32	3.08	102
20	Brunei	ND	ND	ND	ND	ND	ND	ND
21	Papua New Guinea	ND	ND	ND	ND	ND	ND	ND

Source World Bank (2012)

(2019) which in the recent past applied the KAM methodology in a sample of European countries to publish a report on the knowledge economy on that continent and some peripheral regions. Apparently, the Knowledge Economy Index is redundant with the World Economic Forum's Competitiveness Report, published annually since 1979. The 2019 report provides information on 141 economies; the methodology uses four factors subdivided into 12 pillars, which in turn integrate a total of 100 indicators; this set of factors, pillars, and indicators (World Economic Forum, 2019a) include the metrics of the KAM methodology proposed by the World Bank.

For the microeconomic level, knowledge management systems have been developed, defined as information and communication technology platforms that integrate functions for the management of knowledge, tacit, and explicit, between networks of participants in knowledge-intensive business processes; this type of system is intended to support learning and organizational efficiency (Maier, 2007). The main uses of these systems concern the integration of teams of collaborators sharing information, tools, experiences, and technological resources; consumer service and client portfolio management are relevant functions for companies operating these management systems.

Higher education institutions play a leading role in the knowledge economy. According to World Bank data (2020), university enrolment in the world has increased by 394% between 1970 and 2018; Chart 7.1 shows the countries of North America and Europe registering the largest proportions of population with higher education (Roser & Ortiz-Ospina, 2020). The main contributions of higher education to social and economic development are the formation of human capital and research, the dissemination and conservation of knowledge, and the development of practical applications of knowledge. Additionally, in countries with lower levels of development, historically excluded social sectors managed to access higher education, because of a dual-status: demand for citizenship and public policies to expand levels of schooling, with effects that will likely be reflected in the human development indices during the following decades.

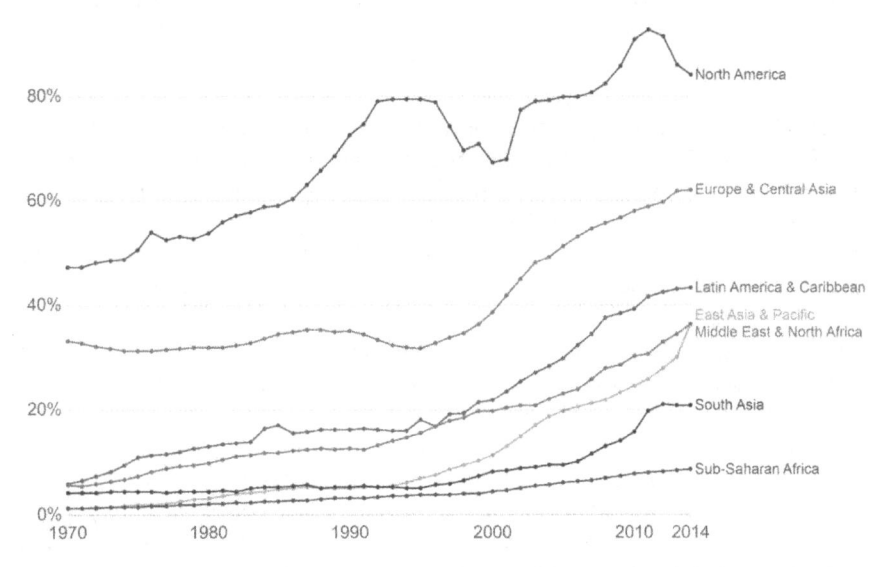

Chart 7.1 Proportion of enrolment in tertiary education (higher, university) (*Source* Roser and Ortiz-Ospina [2020])

Tourism in the Twenty-First Century

Tourism can hardly be considered a novel phenomenon. Holloway (1998) locates its origin in ancient history, mentioning that Naples was already a summer destination among the inhabitants of ancient Rome and that Herodotus narrated how Greek travelers graffitied Egyptian monuments. In the history of tourism, the "Grand Tour" is often remembered, an educational resource in European Enlightenment era among young aristocrats in the process of training as traders, diplomats, or officials, to learn languages and understand the behavior of people from other cultures. At a closer stage, the author discusses the Victorian discourse of rational recreation that drove the development of sun and beach resorts for the English working classes, with successful development until the mid-1960s; their orientation to the working classes led to conceptualize them as mass resorts.

In general, tourism was an activity practiced by the aristocratic and wealthy classes until the end of World War II. The overcrowding of tourism during the second half of the twentieth century is due to a set of various factors, including the economic and demographic explosion after the war. Additionally, the people got more time off, and the jet aircraft was invented, which facilitated long-range travel. Thereafter, the economic and social importance of tourism increased substantially; in some countries it was established as a human right. The study of tourism developed together with the exponential increase of the phenomenon globally.

According to World Tourism Organization (2020), 1.4 billion people traveled abroad during 2018, with an expenditure of $1.45 billion. International tourism has grown at average rates of 5% per year, above the average growth of the world economy, during the past ten years.

Asia-Pacific is the region of the world with the highest growth in visitor flows, with Europe receiving half of the international travelers and the Americas registering the lowest growth rate. The World Tourism Organization only records data from international travelers, as their journeys can be more accurately registered, although international tourism accounts for only about 20% of travel. 80% of the trips correspond to domestic tourism; however, it is not easy to properly follow the local displacements.

During the second half of the twentieth century and the beginning of the nineteenth century, important tourist cities were created, showing the possibility to energize regions formerly marginalized, such as Cancun and Los Cabos, in Mexico, which attracted significant investments and migration flows to deserted regions, with a meager population. Similar cases are featured in Las Vegas, the city that grows the most in the United States and Orlando, Florida, developed around the Disney theme park, with 75 million visitors in 2019; in the Middle East, the city of Dubai became a luxury tourist emporium thanks to large investments from financial surpluses of the oil industry.

Tourism as an industry caught the attention of governments because of the ability to generate substantial income, jobs, and taxes, and because of the potential to boost stagnant regions. That's why tourism is often studied from an economic approach;

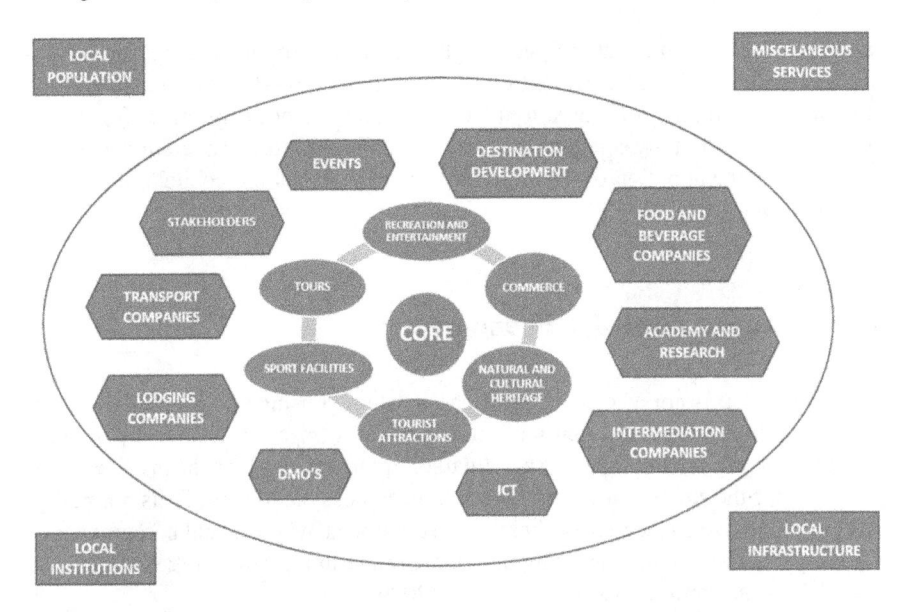

Fig. 7.1 Participants in the tourism industry (*Source* Produced by the authors)

in fact, the currency generated by tourism is considered as exports in the international balance of payments of the countries; although it is rather a multidimensional phenomenon studied from very different disciplines. Tourism is about people moving to places different from their place of residence, carrying out activities different from the daily ones, and the impacts generated by these activities in the receiving destination, although not all travelers are tourists.

Figure 7.1 illustrates the great diversity of factors and actors involved in the tourism phenomenon. In general, the diagram shows that in the center of tourism are tourist attractions, the main reason for people to move from their place of residence to the destination where these are located. Around the arrival of visitors to the location of the attractions the whole group of interested economic actors, such as transport, lodging, food and commerce services, and others, acquire importance. At a higher level exist activities such as management of tourist destinations, planning services, consultancy, and academic and research institutions. Visitor flows generate on the daily lives of receiving communities positive or negative effects. The population, local institutions, and service infrastructure of the town (although not created to serve tourism), are affected, being directly or indirectly interested in the presence of visitors. Similar to the other productive activities, tourism produces a set of environmental, social, and cultural effects at the same time as economic benefits.

The impacts generated by tourism depend on their volume and the kind of travelers visiting a tourist destination. As a multifactorial and diverse phenomenon, a wide range of tourist modalities has developed, such as sun and beach, nature, adventure, cultural, border, dark, black turns, solidarity, cruises, medical, shopping, etc. Similarly, from an academic point of view, tourism has been studied in a multidisciplinary way from the economic, cultural, geographical, and anthropological approaches; in specialized fields, the management of accommodation, food and beverage companies, and the operation of tourist tours are analyzed. Other perspectives frequently used in the tourism study concern the sustainability of the tourism operation, competitiveness and the adoption of information and communication technologies for the management of services.

Tourism and Knowledge Economy

Clearly, tourism is not a science, but it can be studied using the scientific method. In epistemological terms, the current knowledge of tourism presents an incomplete picture of the phenomenon. It is on a pre-paradigmatic stage, which means, there is no paradigm for the study of tourism, nor has it been possible to identify its normality; in general, tourism research studies in a reductionist way particular segments of a more general phenomenon, without achieving the universality of great scientific conceptions. According to Airey and Tribe (2006):

Tourism as a phenomenon is that part of the external world where humans practice the business of being tourists, including that part of the outside world affected by tourism. It is large, messy, complex and dynamic. It covers a range of practices and results. It's not the same as the study of tourism. This latter consists of a research community and a symbolic record of tourism knowledge. It is an attempt by humans to capture, represent, describe, explain and predict the phenomenon of tourism. The study of tourism discovers new ways of contemplating it, traces new concepts, develops new theories and accumulates a body of knowledge. However, tourism knowledge is essentially much less than the activity it describes. It is essentially the business of making generalizations about the phenomenal world of tourism and the packaging of theories (Airey & Tribe, 2006; p. 49).

In the field of public policy, the study of the management of tourist destinations has become relevant for intense international competition for tourism revenue. On the other hand, in the field of technology, Bowen and Whalen (2017) identify the trends with the greatest impact in the field of the global tourism industry: information and communication technologies, data science, social media, the so-called collaborative economy, and robotics for the service. In this sense, the tourism sector is one of the areas of activity that most quickly adopted the applications of information and communication technologies in the areas of business management, marketing, interorganizational linkage, and social communication, integrating the set of applications called e-tourism (Buhalis & Jun, 2011). Table 7.6 shows some of the topics considered central to current tourism research.

The epistemological analysis of tourism takes on meaning for higher education, as it is necessary to define the thematic contents of the tourism curricula at the university level. In general, university studies of tourism present two basic approaches: one of business, or vocational, aimed at preparing students to work professionally in the management and operation of tourist companies of lodging, travel, food and beverage, transport, etc. The second approach is called liberal (Airey & Tribe, 2006), and analyzes the tourist phenomenon and its socioeconomic implications, through disciplines such as sociology, anthropology, cultural heritage, and sustainability, among other topics (Diagram 2). Thus, the first approach is oriented to the business management of tourism, while the second analyzes the tourism phenomenon, especially through the methods of the social sciences. Consequently, the first approach presents a positivist vision and seeks to place graduates in jobs of companies in the field; the second, tends to take critical positions, with the graduates orienting their activities to reflection, research, and teaching of tourism. Often both types of approaches are mixed in the curricula, in greater or lesser proportion; finally, any type of curriculum of professional studies in tourism meets certain ideological criteria (Fig. 7.2).

The image of employment in the tourism sector is contradictory; it is generally valued as an industry that generates numerous jobs, albeit with very low proportion

Table 7.6 Key aspects in the study of tourism

Related to	Dimension
• The tourist.	– Motivation, experience, demand, choice, satisfaction, and interaction
• Business.	– Finance, marketing, human and corporate resources, transportation organization planning, information and communication technologies, hospitality, and recreation
• Receiving community.	– Perceptions of impacts, economic, social, and cultural
• Host environment.	– Ecological and aesthetic impacts
• Host government.	– Measurement of tourism, competitiveness, policies, and planning
• The issuing country.	– Economic, environmental, aesthetic, and sociocultural effects

Source Adapted from Tribe (1999)

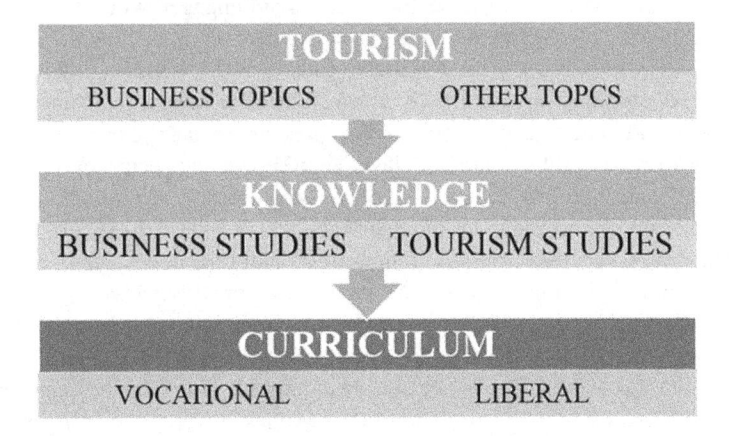

Fig. 7.2 Approaches to the study of tourism (*Source* Adapted from Airey and Tribe [2006])

of human capital, marginal in nature, and with little demand for skills. However, jobs in the industry are highly appreciated by prospective employees, among other reasons, because they are perceived as a mix of work and fun.

Paradoxically, tourist employment presents a glamorous aura, although being considered of low status and minimal preparation. There is a perception of employment involving travel, interpersonal relationships, and multicultural exchanges even working long low-paid days and receiving low training, in low-status jobs. In general, managerial jobs provide prestige, although operational jobs do not; the perception of the status of work in the industry varies in the different areas of the sector: government offices, lodging, travel agencies, transport, and tourist attractions (Vellas, 2016).

Similarly in other areas of economic activity, the vast majority of tourism companies, i.e., more than 95%, are small and medium-sized enterprises (SMEs) that compete with large international corporations of hotels, transport, intermediation, food and beverages, and car rentals, among other fields. Clearly, it is unequal competition, because of the great availability of financial, material, human, and technological resources available to large companies.

While it is true that the competitive advantage of tourism SMEs lies in their ability to provide the specificity and cultural identity in tourist destinations, many of these lack the conditions necessary for the adoption of knowledge management systems, consisting to a great extent of single establishment and family property, without training or management experience. Such SMEs are only interested in adopting and using the instrumental knowledge highly relevant to their operation, a situation that is aggravated by the hiring of part-time and seasonal staff, and high turnover of employees.

In his work on knowledge management systems in tourism, Cooper (2015) notes that the tourism industry arrived late for these methodologies, failing to understand the benefits that knowledge generation and management generate for companies, tourist destinations, and government agencies. Such methodologies are based on the creation, transfer, and application of knowledge in the various organizations, which has not been easy in the tourism sector, as it has not engaged with researchers and the new knowledge they generate. In fact, some authors point out that the companies in the tourism sector as hostile to research (Hudson, 2013; Thomas, 2012).

Knowledge for tourism is defined by Cooper (2015 p. 108) as "… using skills and experience to add intelligence to information in decision-making or provide reliable foundations for action. For tourism, classifying knowledge according to its ability to be coded and therefore communicated is very useful." In tourism companies, most of the knowledge comes from experience and is tacit, not explicit, so it must be coded and recorded in order to communicate and take advantage of it. Knowledge management is important to gain strategic competitive advantages; benefits include improved business processes, boosting innovation, organizational learning and decision-making, streamlining customer response, and the market. Two ways of generating knowledge about tourism are identified: in universities, and through attempts to solve specific field problems in companies, government agencies, and by consultants.

Tourism in the Pacific Basin

Some of the most important countries for global tourism are located in this region; in fact, the world's region with the highest tourism growth today is located in the Pacific Basin. According to information provided by the World Tourism Organization (2020), six of the Pacific Basin countries are among the countries that receive the most tourists or tourism revenues, ranking among the ten countries in the world with the highest tourism activity.

Currency income is an important indicator of tourism competitiveness; in terms of efficiency in the tourism industry, tourist spending is more relevant than the number of visitors (Table 7.7). Tourist spending depends on several factors: among others, the price index of the receiving destination, the quality of the visiting experience, the design of the product, the duration of the visitor's stay, and an efficient application of marketing, especially in terms of segmentation. Table 7.7 shows that Mexico is among the countries that receive a big number of visitors but is not within the first ten places of high tourism revenue; at the opposite end is Australia, which does not receive large flows of visitors, but captures higher average spending per tourist. In terms of foreign exchange acquisition, the United States of America gets the surprising amount of $214 trillion, the amount higher than the GDP of many countries, with tourism as the country's second-largest export industry. According to Table 7.7 some of the most touristic countries in the world, such as France, Italy, and Spain, present a medium performance in terms of receiving tourism revenue.

The World Economic Forum's 2019 Tourism Competitiveness Report assesses the travel and hospitality industry of 140 countries through four indexes, 14 pillars, and 90 indicators. In particular, the report analyzes "the set of factors and policies

Table 7.7 Countries receiving the most visitors and tourism revenue (2019)

N°	Country	Visitors (Millions)	No.	Country	Tourism revenue (Millions of USD)	Average spend per tourist (USD)
1	France	89	1	United States[a]	214,000	2,694
2	Spain	83	2	Spain	74,000	891
3	United States[a]	80	3	France	67,000	753
4	China[a]	63	4	Thailand[a]	63,000	1,647
5	Italy	62	5	United Kingdom	52,000	1,429
6	Turkey	46	6	Italy	49,000	793
7	Mexico[a]	41	7	Australia[a]	45,000	4,778
8	Germany	39	8	Germany	43,000	1,105
9	Thailand[a]	38	9	Japan[a]	41,000	1,318
10	United Kingdom	36	10	China[a]	40,000	642

Source World Tourism Organization (2020)
[a]Pacific Rim countries

Table 7.8 Components of the travel competitiveness index and tourism of the world economic forum

	Indexes			
	Enabling Environment	Conditions of travel policy and national tourism	Infrastructure	Natural and cultural resource
Pillars	• Business environment. • Security • Health and hygiene • Human resources and labor market • Adoption of information and communication technologies	• Priority of travel and tourism • International opening. • Price competitiveness. • Environmental sustainability	• Air transport infrastructure • Port and terrestrial infrastructure. • Tourist services infrastructure	• Natural resources • Cultural resources and business infrastructure

Source World Economic Forum (2019b)

that enable the sustainable development of travel and tourism that in turn contributes to the development and competitiveness of a country."

Table 7.8 shows the indexes and pillars that compose the World Economic Forum's Tourism Competitiveness Index. The subindex facilitating environment includes two pillars that relate directly to the knowledge economy: Human Resources and Labor Market, and Adoption of Information and Communication Technologies.

However, this index also includes another set of factors with great influence on the performance of the tourism industry in countries, including, natural and cultural resources, environmental sustainability, and national tourism policies.

The results of the Global Economic Forum's annual Competitiveness Index do not directly match the results of those countries that record the highest recruitment of visitors and tourism revenues; thus, those countries that attract more tourists and income are not necessarily more competitive. Table 7.9 shows the ranking of tourism competitiveness of economies belonging to the Asia-Pacific Cooperation Mechanism (APEC), taking the results presented in the Travel & Tourism Competitiveness Index (World Economic Forum, 2019b) and adding the results in terms of visitors and tourism revenue published by the World Tourism Organization (2020) (Table 7.9).

In addition, the World Bank's Human Capital Index results are presented in Table 7.9, based on six indicators: probability of survival at age five, expected school years, standardized educational test results, learning by years of adjusted study, children under five years of age, and adult survival rate (World Bank, 2018).

Table 7.9 shows that those countries with higher levels of tertiary education and human capital development are those that record higher levels of tourism competitiveness, tourism income, and average tourist expenditure (without establishing a precise statistical correlation).

7 Higher Education, Knowledge Economy …

Table 7.9 World Economic Forum Travel & Tourism Competitiveness, visitors, tourism revenue, tertiary education, and human capital in APEC member countries

Position index competitiveness World Economic Forum 2019b

	Country	Visitors	Tourism Revenue (million USD)	Average tourist expense (USD)		Tertiary education		Human Capital	
1	Japan[a]	31,192,000	41,115[a]	1,318[a]	1	South Korea[a]	98	Singapore[a]	0.88
2	United States[a]	79,618,000	214,468[a]	2,694[a]	2	Singapore[a]	93	South Korea[a]	0.84
3	Australia[a]	9,426,000	45,035[a]	4,778[a]	3	Australia[a]	90	Japan[a]	0.84
4	Canada[a]	21,134,000	21,936	1,038[a]	4	Chile	88	Hong Kong[a]	0.82
5	China	62,900,000	40,386[a]	642	5	United States[a]	84	Australia[a]	0.8
6	Hong Kong[a]	29,263,000	36,703[a]	1,254[a]	6	Taiwan	83	Canada[a]	0.8
7	South Korea[a]	15,347,000	15,319	998	7	New Zealand[a]	80	New Zealand[a]	0.77
8	Singapore[a]	14,673,000	20,528[a]	1,399[a]	8	Russia Fed.	78	United States[a]	0.76
9	New Zealand[a]	3,686,000	11,004	2,985[a]	9	Hong Kong[a]	70	Russia Fed.	0.73
10	Mexico	41,447,000	22,510	543	10	Japan[a]	62	Chile	0.67
11	Malaysia	25,832,000	19,143	741	11	Thailand	47	China	0.67
12	Thailand	38,277,000	63,042	1,647	12	Brunei	43	Viet Nam	0.67
13	Taiwan	11,067,000	13,704	1,238	13	China	43	Malaysia	0.62
14	Russia Fed.	24,551,000	11,802	481	14	Peru	40	Mexico	0.61
15	Indonesia	13,396,000	1,411	105	15	Philippines	37	Thailand	0.6
16	Peru	4,419,000	3,947	893	16	Indonesia	33	Peru	0.59
17	Chile	5,723,000	2,956	517	17	Mexico	30	Philippines	0.55
18	Viet Nam	15,498,000	10,080	650	18	Viet Nam	30	Indonesia	0.53
19	Brunei	278,000	190	683	19	Malaysia	24	New Guinea	0.38
20	Philippines	7,129,000	7,461	1047	20	Canada	Nd	Taiwan	Nd

(continued)

Table 7.9 (continued)

Position index competitiveness World Economic Forum 2019b

	Country	Visitors	Tourism Revenue (million USD)	Average tourist expense (USD)		Tertiary education		Human Capital
21	New Guinea	Nd	Nd	Nd	21	New Guinea	Nd	Brunei	Nd

[a]Pacific Rim countries

Source Own development with data from World Economic Forum (2019b), World Bank (2018), Asia-Pacific Economic Cooperation (2017), and World Tourism Organization (2020)

Cases of Higher Education in Tourism

Given the impossibility of analyzing all top-level schools in the field of tourism, this document analyzes the cases of three university's schools of tourism from APEC countries, considered paradigmatic because of their relevance in the training of tourism professionals. These are the School of Tourism and Gastronomy of the Autonomous University of the State of Mexico (UAEM), the School of Hotel Management and Tourism of the Hong Kong Polytechnic University, and the Rosen College of Hospitality Management of the University of Central Florida. The last two institutions are located in places one and five in the category of "Management of Hospitality and Tourism" in 2019 by the Academic Ranking of the Universities of the World of Shanghai (Shanghai Ranking Consultancy, 2020); regardless of this classification, both campuses enjoy great recognition in the academic environment of tourism. Unfortunately, not all APEC countries have a higher tourism school registered in that index, e.g., no Latin American and no Southeast Asian country.

The comparative analysis of the three institutions (Table 7.10) shows that Hong Kong and Florida follow a vocational modality, that is, they are oriented to prepare staff for the labor market or for the management of tourist businesses. Meanwhile the Mexican faculty can be considered liberal, as it is more oriented to the analysis

Table 7.10 Comparison between APEC tourism education institutions

Institution		Autonomous University of the State of Mexico	University of Central Florida	Hong Kong Polytechnic University
Foundation		1959	1979	1980
Type of curriculum		Liberal	Vocational	Vocational
Teachers with a PhD		26	58	43
Link		Doesn't mention	Very narrow	School hotel
Academic journals		1 CONACYT	4 JCR	2 JCR
Practice spaces		Doesn't mention	Marriott Laboratories, Disney, Anheuser-Busch	Hotel with its restaurants and bars
Investment in facilities		Doesn't mention	Initial $36 million	6 million euros
Study programs	**Degree**	2	5	2
	Specialty	1	0	0
	Master	2	4	4
	Doctorate	0	1	2
	Training	0	4	2
	Total programs	5	14	10

Source Produced by the authors

of the tourist phenomenon and traditional Mexican gastronomy than to business management.

In terms of teachers with a preferred academic degree for higher education, the Mexican faculty has 26 professors with doctorate, with one important difference: most of these teachers with doctorates do not have training in tourism or business, but their expertise is in education, political science, anthropology, or natural sciences.

Unlike the Mexican institution, the faculties of Hong Kong and the United States publish as meritorious attributes their facilities and laboratories for student practices, their close links with tourism companies, and their continuing education programs for practitioners. In terms of academic journals, the Mexican faculty publishes in best quality research journals in Latin America, although it is not recorded in the journal citation reports.

The institutions of Hong Kong and Orlando illustrate the political will to orient substantial investments to the training of tourism professionals. The areas covered are enabling of laboratories and facilities, recruitment of teachers with doctoral studies, academic research, and linkage with the tourism industry, in line with the approaches of the knowledge economy (Table 7.9).

Discussion and Conclusions

The information analyzed on the countries of the Asia-Pacific Cooperation Mechanism allows inferring that those countries that invest more in higher education, research and development, human capital, and in the factors that compose the knowledge economy are more competitive in international tourism and in their performance in earning income per visitor. Somehow, saying this may seem self-evident, extremely obvious, but it does not seem to be so for the leaders of many countries.

Regarding the relationship between the concepts of knowledge society and the knowledge economy, the characteristics of investment in research and development presented by UNESCO (2018) clearly shows that the conception of the knowledge economy prevails over the knowledge society, especially when most of the resources for this purpose come from private funds. The approaches of Machlup (1962) and Drucker (1969) on research as an industry continue to be in force five decades later, with some countries taking advantage of this evidence and others by inexplicably ignoring it. The theories of Mincer (1958) and Solow (1956) on the role of human capital and the multiplier effect of technology on the development of countries have also not lost importance at present. Unfortunately, knowledge as capital, in an economic sense, reflecting the current state of science, has generated more unequal and divided society (Castelfranchi, 2007; Sörlin & Vessuri, 2007).

Fortunately, the World Bank (2007) developed methodologies to foster the knowledge economy applied with positive results in countries such as Ireland, Finland, and South Korea. It would be recommendable to generate more publications and documents on the results obtained in the economies of these countries.

In the context of the society and the knowledge economy, universities are crucial actors in the training of professionals, the generation of human capital, and the production of knowledge through research activities. The information provided by Roser and Ortiz-Ospina (2020) highlights the coverage of North America and Europe in university population, in line with investment in research and development and tourism competitiveness.

The global tourism has presented exponential growth between the second half of the twentieth century and today, acquiring more economic and cultural importance, promoting the redistribution of income and cultural exchanges. However, because of its character as a multifactorial and dynamic phenomenon, it has not been possible until now to generate a scientific model that allows explaining and understanding its nature, without having a theoretical paradigm that understands its study (Airey & Tribe, 2006). On the other hand, Hudson (2013), Thomas (2012), and Cooper (2015) point out some reluctance of tourism companies to adopt and manage knowledge. In this same sense, Bowen and Whalen (2017) and Buhalis and Jun (2011) mention the great relevance that information and communication technologies have for the tourism industry. However, Hjalager (2015) highlights that those innovations that have historically had the greatest impact on tourism activity have been generated in other fields of activity and have been adopted in tourism, without having emerged to the interior of the industry.

The results of the tourism industry in attracting visitors and tourism revenues among the countries of the Asia-Pacific Cooperation Mechanism reveal that some of them are among the ten most prominent, based on data from the World Tourism Organization (2020). According to information provided in the Travel & Tourism Competitiveness Report 2019 (World Economic Forum, 2019b). APEC's ten most competitive countries are the same countries that invest the most in research and development and have greater coverage in tertiary education, higher levels of human capital. It is inferred from these that greater tertiary education, greater development of human capital, and greater investment in research and development have an impact on higher tourism competitiveness and greater use per visitor received.

As for the characteristics of higher education for tourism, it is necessary to emphasize the importance of approach and quality to strengthen the approach of the knowledge society. The review of three tourism education institutions in Mexico, Hong Kong, and the United States of America highlights the need for high-level teachers, preferential degree and industry-specific training, substantial investments in practice spaces and laboratories, as well as close ties to industry. That is, an approach to the tourism business in tan-torque with the willingness and political will to invest in higher education in the field of tourism.

References

Airey, D., & Tribe, J. (2006). *An international handbook of tourism education*. Routledge.
Asia-Pacific Economic Cooperation. (2017). *APEC ECONOMIC POLICY REPORT 2017 structural reform and human capital development*. Asia-Pacific Economic Cooperation Secretariat.
Bell, D. (1973). *The coming of post-industrial society*. Basic Books.
Bowen, J., & Whalen, E. (2017). Trends that are changing travel and tourism. *Worldwide Hospitality and Tourism Themes*. https://www.researchgate.net/deref/http%3A%2F%2Fdx.doi.org%2F10.1108%2FWHATT-09-2017-0045.
Buhalis, D., & Jun, S. H. (2011). E-tourism. *Contemporary tourism reviews, 1*, 2–38.
Castelfranchi, C. (2007). Six critical remarks on science and the construction of the knowledge society. *Journal of Science Communication, 6*(4), C03.
Chen, D. H., & Dahlman, C. J. (2005). *The knowledge economy, the KAM methodology and World Bank operations* (World Bank Institute Working Paper).https://documents.worldbank.org/pt/publication/documents-reports/documentdetail/695211468153873436/the-knowledge-economy-the-kam-methodology-and-world-bank-operations.
Cooper, C. (2015). Managing tourism knowledge. *Tourism Recreation Research, 40*(1), 107–119.
Drucker, P. (1969). *The age of discontinuity: Guidelines to our changing society*. Routledge.
European Bank for Reconstruction and Development. (2019). *Introducing the EBRD knowledge economy index*. London. file:///E:/LIBRO%20APEC%20USB/ebrd-knowledge-economy-index.pdf.
Hjalager, A. M. (2015). 100 innovations that transformed tourism. *Journal of Travel Research, 54*(1), 3–21.
Holloway, J. (1998). *The business of tourism*. New York: Addison Wesley Longman.
Hudson, S. (2013). Knowledge exchange: A destination perspective. *Journal of Destination Marketing and Management, 2*(3), 129–131.
Machlup, F. (1962). *The production and distribution of knowledge in the United States*. Princeton University Press.
Maier, Ronald. (2007). *Knowledge management systems: information and communication technologies for knowledge management*. Berlin Heidelberg: Springer-Verlag.
Mincer, J. (1958). Investment in human capital and personal income distribution. *Journal of Political Economy, 66*(4).
Our World in Data. (2020). https://ourworldindata.org/entries-by-year/2020.
Rooney, D., Hearn, G., & Ninan, A. (2005). Knowledge: Concepts, policy, implementation. *Handbook on the knowledge economy* (pp. 1–18).
Roser, M., & Ortiz-Ospina, E. (2020). *Tertiary education*. Published online at OurWorldInData.org. https://ourworldindata.org/tertiary-education.
Shanghai Ranking Consultancy. (2020). *Academic Ranking of World Universities*. Shanghai Ranking's Global Ranking of Academic Subjects 2019—Hospitality & Tourism Management. http://www.shanghairanking.com/Shanghairanking-Subject-Rankings/hospitality-tourism-management.html.
Solow, R. M. A. (1956). Contribution to the theory of growth. *The Quarterly Journal of Economics, 70*(1), 65–94.
Sörlin, S., & Vessuri, H. (2007). *Knowledge society vs. knowledge economy. Knowledge, power, and politics*. Springer.
Statista. (2020). *The 100 largest companies in the world by market value in 2019*. Statista. https://www.statista.com/statistics/263264/top-companies-in-the-world-by-market-value/.
Thomas, R. (2012). Business elites, universities and knowledge transfer in tourism. *Tourism Management, 33*(3), 553–561.
Tribe, J. (1999). The concept of tourism: Framing a wide tourism world and broad tourism society. *Tourism Recreation Research, 22*(2), 75–81.

United Nations Education, Science and Culture Organization (UNESCO). (2018). *Global investments in R&D* http://uis.unesco.org/sites/default/files/documents/fs50-global-investments-rd-2018-en.pdf.

Vellas, F. (2016). *The international marketing of travel and tourism: A strategic approach.* Macmillan International Higher Education.

World Bank. (2007). Building knowledge economies: Advanced strategies for development. World Bank. https://openknowledge.worldbank.org/handle/10986/6853.

World Bank. (2012). *Knowledge economic index.* http://web.worldbank.org/archive/website01030/WEB/IMAGES/KAM_V4.PDF.

World Bank. (2018). *Human capital index and components, 2018.* https://www.worldbank.org/en/data/interactive/2018/10/18/human-capital-index-and-components-2018.

World Bank. (2020). *World Bank School enrollment, tertiary (% gross)* https://data.worldbank.org/indicator/SE.TER.ENRR?end=2018&start=1970&view=chart.

World Economic Forum. (2019a). *The global competitiveness report 2019. Geneva:* WEF.http://www3.weforum.org/docs/WEF_TheGlobalCompetitivenessReport2019.pdf.

World Economic Forum. (2019b). *The travel & tourism competitiveness Report 2019.* The World Economic Forum. WEF.https://www.weforum.org/reports/the-travel-tourism-competitiveness-report-2019.

World Tourism Organization. (2020). *International tourism highlights 2019.*

World Tourism Organization. https://www.e-unwto.org/doi/pdf/10.18111/9789284421152.

Chapter 8
Business and Training in a Knowledge-Based Economy Environment: The Telmex Case

Leticia Reyes Morin

Abstract In the Knowledge-Based Economy, a system where knowledge is the true essence of competitiveness and the engine of long-term development, education is not limited to institutionalized training, but requires lifelong learning, which is being built outside educational institutions, especially in the most avant-garde companies, which consider it a fundamental asset for their development and growth. Companies participate in the creation of knowledge, since a characteristic of the Knowledge-Based Economy is the diversity of actors. Higher Education Institutions (HEI) are also bridges of interaction between the various factors of economic activity, providing the human resources that the labor market demands. This chapter outlines the case of *Teléfonos de México* (Telmex) and its Corporate University (Technological Institute of *Teléfonos de México*, Inttelmex), which since 1990 has undertaken an arduous process of technological modernization and training of its human resources, in order to provide them with labor competencies, and allow them to face the challenge of global competitiveness and the development of new telecommunications services in an emerging economy within the Pacific Rim. We conclude that education and the development of labor competencies are not the sole responsibility of HEIs. It is a responsibility shared with employers and governments, through education policies, international organizations, and agreements, to consolidate programs that guide countries to generate equity on local, national, and international level.

Introduction

In the Knowledge-Based Economy, a system where knowledge is the true essence of competitiveness and the engine of long-term development, education is not limited to institutionalized training, but requires lifelong learning, which is being built outside educational institutions, especially in the most avant-garde companies, which consider it a fundamental asset for their development and growth.

L. Reyes Morin (✉)
Grupo Carso, México City, México

© The Author(s), under exclusive license to Springer Nature Singapore Pte Ltd. 2021
J. E. Rangel Delgado and A. Ivanova Boncheva (eds.), *Knowledge Society and Education in the Asia-Pacific*, SpringerBriefs in Education,
https://doi.org/10.1007/978-981-16-2333-2_8

Companies participate in the creation of knowledge, since a characteristic of the Knowledge-Based Economy is the diversity of actors. Higher Education Institutions (HEI) are also bridges of interaction between the various factors of economic activity, providing the human resources that the labor market demands.

This essay outlines the case of *Teléfonos de México* (Telmex) and its Corporate University (Technological Institute of *Teléfonos de México*, Inttelmex), which since 1990 have undertaken an arduous process of technological modernization and training of its human resources, in order to provide them with labor competencies that will allow them to face the challenge of global competitiveness and the development of new telecommunication services in an emerging economy country as part of the Pacific Rim.

It is emphasized that, at least in the case of Mexican companies, there is little awareness of the importance of developing labor competencies to face the challenges of the Knowledge-Based Economy.

It is emphasized that education and the development of labor competencies are not the sole responsibility of HEIs. It is a responsibility shared with employers and governments, through education policies, international organizations, and agreements, to consolidate programs that guide countries to generate equity in local, national, and international economic development and growth.

Knowledge Society and Knowledge-Based Economy

The development of Information and Communication Technologies (ICT) has impacted the form of communication, coexistence, economic production, and social organization. Particularly in the field of education, ICTs have transformed the teaching-learning process, obliging all participants to review the designs of education systems at various levels, to generate new policies for coverage and access to the media, and to give way to structured mechanisms for linking with the changing reality demanded by society.

The proliferation of ICTs has also forced to rethinking of the right to education, from its institutionalization to access to the media, as a mechanism for inclusion of individuals in a globalized world.

The Knowledge Society, in which we find ourselves, "envisions a social and economic development based on processes of sharing people's knowledge to create value and innovations (learning processes) that translate into products and services, and in short, well-being for the citizen" (Arboniés, 2006, p. 26).

On the matter, Castells (1999, p. 63) states: "What characterizes the current technological revolution is not the centrality of knowledge and information, but the application of that knowledge and information, knowledge generation and information/communication processing devices, in a circle of cumulative feedback between innovation and its uses," and he notes: "The spread of technology infinitely amplifies its power by appropriating it and redefining its users. The new information technologies are not just tools to be applied, but processes to be developed. For the first time in history, the human mind is a direct productive force, not just a decisive element of the production system" (Castells, 1999, p. 63).

For Courrier (2000), when talking about the Information Society, the emphasis is on the content of the work (the process of capturing, processing, and communicating the necessary information), while the Knowledge Society places it on the economic agents, who must have higher qualifications to carry out their work.

However, the increase in the rate of creation, accumulation, and use of knowledge has led today's societies toward a new paradigm known as the Knowledge-Based Economy: a system where knowledge is the true essence of competitiveness and the engine of long-term development (Facultad Latinoamericana de Ciencias Sociales, 2006).

The main pillars of this phase are national education and training, infrastructure for access to information and telecommunications, innovation by companies, universities, and research centers, as well as investment in science and technology, which allow the use and application of knowledge for the growth and development of countries.

Thus, knowledge is not limited to institutionalized training, but is evolving toward lifelong learning, which is being built outside educational institutions, especially in the most avant-garde companies, which consider it a fundamental asset for their development and growth.

Companies participate this way in the creation of knowledge, since a characteristic of the Knowledge-Based Economy is the diversity of actors. In this sense, for the educational systems of the nations, but above all for Higher Education Institutions (HEI), in the Knowledge Society and the Knowledge-Based Economy, the great challenge is represented by the speed with which such information is generated, transmitted, and processed to become knowledge.

But not only that, the HEIs are also bridges of interaction between the various factors of economic activity, by providing the human resources demanded by the labor market, with new and increasingly specialized and changing skills of international quality (Fig. 8.1).

Wang (2008), proposes that, in order for universities and institutes of higher education to contribute to human development and social mobility, they must be within reach and open to all individuals who want to learn and continue learning, through teaching models such as open and distance learning, dual or mixed type universities, and universities of entrepreneurs.

In other words, models where the common denominator is flexibility and open access to the population, with a new educational philosophy in the form of management and administration scholarships consequently also changes in the role of students and teachers, renewal of curricula, review of content, and relevance of the same to improve skills, communication and interdisciplinary skills, entrepreneurship, in order to train them for the demand of changing labor markets, internationalization of HEIs through knowledge of the diversity of cultures, professional specialization, and mastery of information and communication technologies (Wang, 2008).

The Knowledge Society and the Knowledge-Based Economy place varying demands on nations to grow and exploit their competitive advantages. In the global

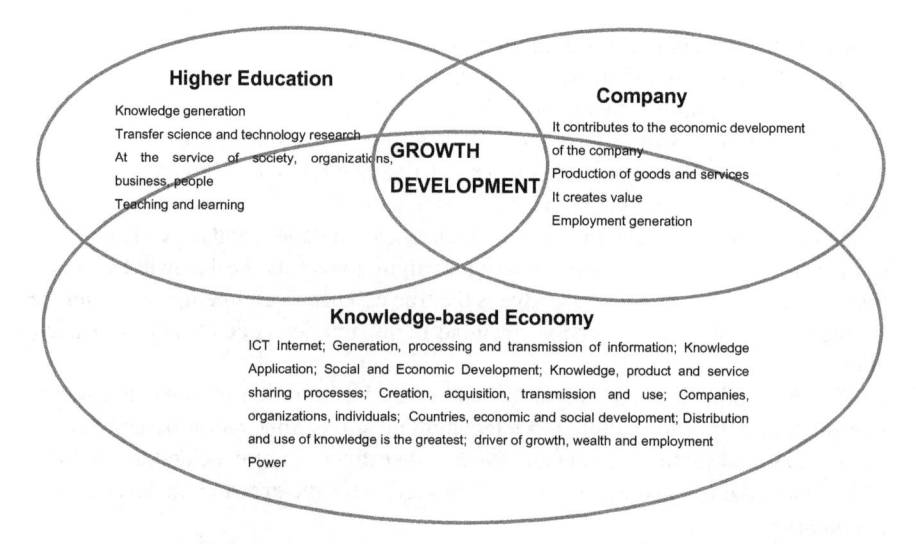

Fig. 8.1 Dynamic development model *Source* Own elaboration

context, the region formed by the countries of the Pacific Rim is fundamental. Due to its location and geographical area, it has a decisive weight in the world economy, since 50% of the world's total population is concentrated there, constituting a gigantic consumer and producer market. Together, the more than 40 countries located in the region account for approximately 47% of the world's gross product and concentrate around 37% of total exports exchanged on the planet.

Among these nations is Mexico, the eleventh largest economy in the world, according to its Gross Domestic Product (GDP). Its geographical location, especially its border with the second-largest economy in the world (the United States), provides it with privileged opportunities, which have not necessarily been taken advantage of by the country's governments to try to place themselves in the context of the Knowledge Society and the Knowledge-Based Economy.

To exemplify an area in which Mexico has stood out notably, we will take the case of Telmex, a parastatal company that was privatized by the government in 1990 and that had to modernize rapidly to face a competitive environment, not only national but also international, because it had to contend in highly competitive markets with large global companies, and for this it had to modernize not only the technology but, above all, train its workforce (almost 50,000 employees in 1990) in record time, in order to equip it with the necessary skills and to face the new environment.

Skills in the Knowledge Society

The obvious question is: What skills are needed to participate in the Knowledge Society?

There is a diversity of typologies and classifications of competencies, since it is a multimodal concept that is made up of behavior, personality, knowledge, and attitude aspects to demonstrate that one has the capacity to carry out an activity or solve a problem in a given context.

There are initiatives and concrete proposals to implement educational evaluation practices of competencies, which respond to the need to generate a methodology of analysis. One of them is the DeSeCo Project (Definition and Selection of Competencies) of the Organization for Economic Cooperation and Development (OECD), which defines and selects a group of competencies that are essential for the life of individuals and the proper functioning of society (Reynoso, 2007).

Another initiative is the Tuning Project, dedicated to the analysis of the comparability and compatibility of professional training among European universities, where it defines the competencies associated with professional training (Reynoso, 2007) (Table 8.1).

Mexico has the National System of Competencies (NSC), a government agency that seeks to contribute to Mexico's economic competitiveness, educational development, and social progress by strengthening people's skills. The National System of Competencies provides information on skill level standards required by Mexican entrepreneurs, workers, teachers, and public officials, with the aim of "facing the challenges that the globalized market demands." Organizational development and quality, sales through sectoral competence management committees, the competence profiles of human capital in the various productive and service sectors of the country are defined (CONOCER, 2019a).

NSC has a National Registry of Competency Standards, which is the national reference for the evaluation and certification of people's competencies, which describe

Table 8.1 Competencies that are considered critical in the assessment of higher education

Generics		Instrumental: cognitive, methodological, technology, linguistic	– Analysis and synthesis capacity – Knowledge of a foreign language – Decision-making capacity
		Interpersonal: individual and social	– Critical thinking – Teamwork – Ethical commitment
		Systemic or integrative	Creativity – Leadership – Self-employment
Specific competencies		Disciplinary and academic (knowledge)	– Basic general knowledge
		Professionals (know-how)	– Project development and management

Source Reynoso (2007)

the set of knowledge, skills, abilities, and attitudes that a person must have in order to execute a work activity with a high level of performance.

Based on evidence portfolios and certification processes, the National Council for Standardization and Certification of Labour Competencies (CONOCER) evaluates and certifies in coordination with business or workers' associations, public or private institutions, which comply with the process established by the body.

NSC seeks to promote the quality of the country's labor and business force, thus strengthening the productivity and growth capacity of companies by having a quality reference in the current environment of the knowledge economy.

An important aspect is that NSC facilitates the labor mobility of workers in their sectors, since the country's educational authority recognizes their skills through a certificate granted jointly by the Ministry of Public Education and CONOCER.

CONOCER (2019b) applies an Annual Survey on Skills in Mexico, whose objective is to obtain relevant information on the degree of penetration and application of skills models in the country. The 2017 survey report contains relevant results for our study:

- Six out of ten organizations do not use the labor competencies approach in their processes.
- There is an incipient understanding of the functioning, objectives, benefits, and operation mechanisms of NSC in organizations, especially among small- and medium-sized companies of national origin.
- The larger companies—with predominantly foreign capital and from the social sector—the use of labor competencies rises significantly, from 40.7 to 75%. at larger companies with predominantly foreign capital and from the public sector
- The organizational and managerial competencies most valued by organizations are strategic planning, integration of work teams, and marketing, effective communication, leadership, administrative efficiency, strategic and business vision, as well as knowledge and change management.
- Among the technical competencies, updating, mastering processes, and quality assurance stand out.
- The most outstanding social–emotional competencies are empathy and companionship, self-regulation and motivation, as well as quality of service.
- The most valued competencies in the organizations are communication, marketing, and digital advertising; knowledge of languages and last generation platforms; industry 4.0; social networks and marketing.
- The most relevant transversal competencies were teamwork, quality, planning and organization, responsibility, effective communication, leadership, commitment, customer service, results orientation, and decision-making.
- The use of labor competencies in organizations contributes to improvements in productivity, since 68.9% of the organizations that use the CONOCER model or another competencies model registered an increase in productivity with respect to three previous years.
- Only 10% of companies use labor competencies as a system of management and continuous improvement

Among the main difficulties faced by organizations in the use of competency standards, 44.1% point out a lack of connection between standards and the processes and particular needs of their own organization.

This fact reflects the aspiration of organizations to have standards that emanate directly from their processes and the difficulty of summarizing in a standard the performance criteria at the branch or industry level.

In terms of certification, the main problems pointed out by organizations are the lack of knowledge of how certification works by companies, with 44.1%; followed by personnel turnover, with 38.2%.

The above invites us to identify the lack of communication and articulation that exists between the regulatory bodies in competencies and the companies. The benefits for companies should be disseminated and they should be aware of the mechanisms for the management of knowledge, skills, and attitudes required by each branch of industry.

The Telmex Case

The case of Telmex is paradigmatic to understand the problems of companies in emerging countries in terms of training their human resources, to meet the challenges posed by the changing reality of a Knowledge-based Economy.

In 1990, the Mexican government decided to put up for sale Telmex, the second most important parastatal company after *Petróleos Mexicanos* (Pemex), as part of the national modernization program. The winner of the sale was an international conglomerate led by *Grupo Carso*, with South Western Bell International Holdings of the United States and France Cable et Radio (France Telecom) as technology partners.

The government established a regulatory regime based on a new Telmex Concession Title, which set goals that the new owners were required to meet in a timely manner to retain the concession.

These were some of the goals: investments of more than 24 billion pesos for modernization and expansion of infrastructure; incorporation of 2.3 million telephone lines to reach 7.5 in 1993; providing telephone services to almost 8 thousand rural communities of more than 500 inhabitants, which would represent an increase of 77% with respect to the total number of populations in service in 1990, and doubling the number of public telephones in operation, and building a 13,500-kilometer fiber-optic network.

In this way, Telmex proposed to raise service standards to international levels within seven years.

In addition, Telmex would have to face the opening of competition in long-distance services by the end of 1993. It was obliged to present an interconnection plan between public networks, which was a requirement for potentially interested parties to offer the telecommunications service (Alestra, 2006).

Telmex had 49,912 employees in 1990 and made significant organizational changes to meet the demands of the government and the competitive environment, both at the management level and in terms of organizational structure, personnel rules and policies, leadership style, teamwork, and, above all, to modify old practices of a government company to make it a customer-centric company, in the provision of value-added services.

In order to achieve these goals, Telmex set out as strategies:

- Strengthen leadership in traditional markets
- Focus on value-added products and services
- Expansion into foreign markets
- Healthy financial situation
- Training of personnel.

The Inttelmex Corporate University Model

The Mexican government established a requirement for the new owners of Telmex to include workers in the modernization process, as well as to avoid layoffs and to propose a comprehensive training program.

As part of the agreements established in the Collective Labor Agreement (CCT) with the Telephone Operators' Union of the Mexican Republic (STRM), the *Instituto Tecnológico de Teléfonos de México S.C.* was created in 1991 (Inttelmex), which would carry out the corporate strategy to face the challenge of training and education of personnel, with modern methods and systems of educational technology and evaluation, test workshops, models, laboratories, and research and development centers.

Inttelmex, which conformed to the corporate university model, established as its fundamental objectives:

- To modernize human capital and turn it into a force internationally competitive.
- Addressing the needs of training, education, development, and education.
- Anticipate changes in information and communication technologies and the impact on human resource development.

In coordination with STRM, the company and Inttelmex committed to develop, implement, and update a General Training System (GTS), where the needs of modernization, digitalization, new services, and products were established, as well as to professionalize the workers both in their specialty and in their productive area; to raise the level of medium-higher and professional studies of the workers, and the training of human resources for research and development of own technology.

The GTS is made up of the following subsystems:

- Analysis of activities, what each job does.
- Training profiles, knowledge, basic skills, and expected attitudes per position.
- General programs, specialty curriculum for on-the-job performance.

- Identifying training needs.
- Standardization and certification of labor competence, in coordination with CONOCER.
- Training operation, follow-up, and control of training programs, through the physical infrastructure of the Operation Campuses and the educational platforms such as Inttelmex Virtual.
- Evaluation of training, measurement of training results to feed back into the process, and develop indicators.
- Instructor-designers of courses, ensure that those who design or deliver the training are qualified to perform these functions.
- Open education systems, formal education programs for workers.
- Training history.
- Professional development plans.
- Free courses.
- Development plans for technology assimilation and transfer, to train human resources specialized in technology assimilation and transfer.

The General Training System (GTS) was based on the development of educational technology and training evaluation methodologies in order to identify training needs and requirements.

Profiles and job levels were reviewed by specialty of work for unionized personnel, through the methodology of functional analysis, and performance responsibilities were determined.

In conjunction with the profiles and job levels of the unionized personnel, the competencies were determined for the corporate personnel according to the job level: director, first-level management, middle management, personnel without command, and positions with unionized personnel in charge; thus covering all the specialties and corporate areas of the company.

The main competencies that were determined for the personnel, according to the level of the position were (Table 8.2).

In the first years of operation of Inttelmex (1991–1994), the topics of training and education were focused on technological leveling courses, and from 1995 on, training for the process of interconnection of new long-distance operators, customer service, sales and marketing, and specialization in the technical, commercial, and administrative areas (Wilde, 1998).

The main training programs that were developed were:

- Administration.
- Management and Business.
- Marketing, Customer Service.
- Product Development.
- Engineering Development.
- Information Technologies.
- Human Development.
- Training Programs (Specialization, Diplomas, Masters, and Certifications).
- New Technology in the Industry.

Table 8.2 Knowledge, skills, and attitudes requited by job level

Job Level	Competencies
Management Managers	• Guide teamwork • Communication • Participate as a team member • Applies the Company's interrelationships • Results- and cost-oriented • Customer-oriented • It aims at improvement • Innovation • Use of ICT • Lead the change
Non-commanded personnel	• Participate as a team member • Communication • Results and profitability oriented • Applies the Company's interrelationships • Adapts to change • It focuses on satisfaction and customer service • Creativity • Proposes solutions

Source Own elaboration

Inttelmex Training Evaluation Model

Since 2001, Inttelmex implemented the Training Quality System, in order to feed back the process for a continuous improvement according to ISO 9001:2000 requirements. Inttelmex permanently reviews the teaching and learning models to respond to the cognitive processes demanded by the knowledge society.

Below, we show how Inttelmex training models evolved, in terms of educational technology as part of the process of permanent updating of teaching-learning processes (Table 8.3).

The model of educational technology, Connectivism, as proposed by Stephen Downes and George Siemens, is the theory of learning for the digital age. It is complex learning in a rapidly evolving digital social world through technologies and networks, learning occurs through connections within networks of nodes (Eduarea, 2014).

At the same time, the evolution of training models determined the adequacy and adjustment of evaluation models for training and education programs.

Inttelmex's Training Evaluation Model (MEC in Spanish words) was defined as a continuous and permanent process that would allow for the monitoring of both training programs and learning processes, in order to issue criteria or judgments that allowed for immediate, timely, and accessible decision-making.

Table 8.3 Chronology of the evolution of Inttelmex Instructional Design Models

Instructional design	Behavioral by objectives 1991	New cognitive behavioral approach NEC 2005	Training evolution constructivist EVOCAP 2010	Competency-based approach DIC 2014–2016	Social constructivist 2016–2019
Methodology	Specific objectives by conduct Stimulus-response Pre-established evaluation criteria With the methodology of functional analysis the open systems instructional skills workshop	Open systems employee involvement Process and product entry Active process builds learning from experience	Significant knowledge Participation Learning Environments Structuring and sequence to facilitate Constructivist processing Collaborative practice Participant centered intervention	Knowledge through experience Meaningful, holistic, and collaborative learning Competencies Design and development by competencies Know-how	To use ICT and learning Learning Platforms Technology as a medium Pedagogical Dimension Eclectic Models Design and development by performance Micro classes
Theoretical support	Behaviorism	Systems theories	Cognitivism	Constructivist and systems	Connectivism

Source Own elaboration

The training evaluation model adopted, at least in its structure, was that of Kirkpatrik (1999), since Inttelmex developed its own instruments and tools for each level of evaluation (Table 8.4).

The Training Evaluation Model objective is to measure the effectiveness of training toward a competitive approach, so it moved from obtaining qualifications to generating indicators that would provide information for decision-making in the training process as a whole, as a process of continuous improvement.

Links with the HEIs: Pending Bill

It should be noted that during the accelerated phase of Telmex's modernization process described above, Inttelmex did not have much interaction with national or international HEIs. Even though it is true that a good part of the professionals working in the company were trained in the country's public and private universities, most of the staff (especially the unionized ones) obtained their labor preparation in the classrooms of Inttelmex.

It was not until years later that collaboration agreements were established with the National Autonomous University of Mexico (UNAM in Spanish words), the National Polytechnic Institute (IPN in Spanish words), the International University

Table 8.4 Training evaluation levels and factors

Evaluation level	Evaluation factors
Level One Reaction Training Event Satisfaction	• Level of satisfaction that participants have, at the end of a training event: content, training materials, facilitation, equipment, facilities, instructor, and the learning environment
Level Two Learning	• Level of mastery of knowledge before and after the course, competencies for which the course was designed • Acquisition of new knowledge and development of new skills • It consists of the evaluation at three different moments: before the event (Diagnostic), during (Formative), and after (Summative)
Level Three Job Application Tracking	• Level of application and transfer of knowledge and skills in the workplace • Frequency, time of application, factors that facilitate the application, conditions for application, relevance, and the level of linkage with the Productive Indicators of the position.
Level Four Contribution to Strategies	• Level of impact on results in the work area, contribution to quality and productivity in the work areas according to the company's strategies

Source Own elaboration

of La Rioja in Mexico (UNIR Mexico, in Spanish Words), and the Massachusetts Institute of Technology (MIT) to generate alliances in technology and education.

On the other hand, through the Telmex-Telcel Foundation, scholarship programs were carried out for higher education students, a mechanism that serves to identify the best students and graduates from the HEIs to incorporate them into Telmex and other *Grupo Carso* companies. To date, it has given scholarships to nearly 380,000 people throughout the country.

Inttelmex IT (Inttelmex Information Technology) was created as part of the *"Telmex Impulso a la Innovación Tecnológica"* initiative, which is a Training and Development Center for Top Management for Information Technology professionals. More than 1,200 companies, 15,073 professionals, and 154 teachers in administration have participated in this project (UNIR, 2018).

Similarly, academic was designed, which is an interactive platform, which brings together educational content from recognized HEIs and International Research Centers, with the aim of sharing knowledge and making it accessible to everyone who wants to learn and develop their potential, especially the less advantaged sectors (UNIR, 2018).

Final Comments

Since its privatization, Telmex faced the challenge of transforming from an analog technology company to a digital organization, typical of the Knowledge Society, even before this concept proliferated in the economic, academic, and business environment, where the mastery of skills by employees was the key to creativity, innovation, and knowledge management.

But today Telmex faces other challenges to survive in the globalized world. The technological and human modernization was more than fulfilled, but the current reality poses new imperatives.

The case of Telmex is paradigmatic of the situation in which companies in emerging economies face the challenges of the Knowledge Society. A key element was investment in training and education; renewal of technological infrastructure; use of information technologies as support for innovation, as well as alliances and collaboration agreements with business partners.

Through Inttelmex, the company was able to develop its own strategies to train personnel in the required skills in several phases: first, in the transition from a telephone company to a telecommunications company, then to an information and communications technology company, and now as a network infrastructure company. Providing a sort of pairing between KBE Knowledge-Based Economy and the KBS Knowledge Society that is expressed in KES skills in the knowledge-based economy.

Telmex implemented a strategy of change in the organizational culture of the employees, in the way they perceive their work, in the value chain, in the fulfillment of goals, results, quality, productivity, and the way they serve the customer. Training as an educational action was transforming in the company: learning, and learning to learn, taking into account the work experience and incorporating new learning into the change process.

The case of Telmex shows that it was necessary to use its own human resources to design, implement, and evaluate the training strategy in the competencies, and thus give an immediate response to the change.

In this sense, the HEIs did not participate directly in the process, since they could not respond to the rapid and drastic change demanded by the company and its environment.

In fact, HEIs are the fundamental axis for training and professionalizing human resources in competencies, knowledge, skills, and attitudes to face challenges. There are international and national initiatives to evaluate the way in which HEIs contribute to the formation of competencies, but they have not been sufficient.

Better mechanisms of articulation between HEIs and enterprises must be generated in order to anticipate the changes demanded by the national and global scenario in the Knowledge Economy Society, especially in countries like Mexico.

In this articulation of efforts, should be included as the normative reference for the updating and quality of the performance of the competencies of the employees for their accreditation and certification. Let's not forget that CONOCER is part of the network of Inter-American Centre for the Development of Knowledge in Vocational

Training (ILO/Cinterfor) denominator that raises the standard of the competencies, always thinking of promoting the competitiveness of the labor and business force of the country, as well as of the workers of the social sector and the government.

Education and the development of labor competencies is not the sole responsibility of HEIs. It is a responsibility shared with employers and governments, through education policies, international organizations, and agreements, to consolidate programs that guide countries to generate equity in local, national, and international economic development and growth.

For Telmex and Inttelmex it was clear that the pillars of investment, innovation, and vision were fundamental to achieve results: investment in training and the formation of the competencies required by the market.

There is much to be done within the companies to potentialize the competencies of their human resources, and in each HEI to analyze if they are responding to the demand for training of international professionals with the quality that the global environment demands.

References

Alestra. (2006). *Estar cerca Crónica Testimonial de una Década de Alestra*. L&L Ediciones Imagen y Promoción Cultural S.C.

Arboniés, O. A. L. (2006). *Conocimiento para Innovar*, cómo evitar la miopía en la gestión de conocimiento. Díaz de Santos.

Castells, M. (1999). La era de la información. Revista de Ciencias Políticas. *Politeia, 29,* 230–233. https://www.redalyc.org/articulo.oa?id=1700/170033587012.

CONOCER. (2019a). *Sistema Nacional de Competencias*. https://conocer.gob.mx/acciones_programas/sistema-nacional-competencias/.

CONOCER. (2019b). *Encuesta anual sobre competencias en México. Informe de resultados 2017*. https://conocer.gob.mx/documentos/encuesta-anual-sobre-competencias-en-mexico-informe-de-resultados-2017/.

Courrier, Y. (2000). *Societé de l'Information et Technologies*, UNESCO. Web News, Point of View, Archives. http://www.unesco.org/webworld/poin.

Eduarea. (2014). *¿Qué es el conectivismo? Teoría del Aprendizaje para la Era Digital*. Eduarea's Blog. https://eduarea.wordpress.com/2014/03/19/que-es-el-conectivismo-teoria-del-aprendizaje-para-la-era-digital/.

Facultad latinoamericana de Ciencias sociales. (2006). Programa de investigación sobre economía del conocimiento en América Latina y el Caribe FLACSO; Centro Internacional de Investigaciones para el desarrollo de Canadá (p. 7). http://blog.utp.edu.co/plandcti/.

Kirkpatrick, D. L. (1999). *Evaluación de Acciones Formativas: Los Cuatro Niveles*. Gestión 2000.

Reynoso, A. R. (2007). *Exámenes de Habilidades Profesionales para Carreras Profesionales afines: Características generales y posibilidades de desarrollo*. http://www.ceneval.edu.mx/.

UNIR La Universidad en Internet. (2018). *UNIR México firma alianza con Telmex – Académica*. https://mexico.unir.net/vive-unir/unir-mexico-firma-alianza-con-telmex-academica/.

Wang, Y. (2008). *Educación Superior para el Desarrollo Humano y Social en Asia y el Pacífico. Nuevos desafíos y roles cambiantes*. Universitat Politecnica de Cataluya Barcelona Tech. https://upcommons.upc.edu/handle/2099/7935.

Wilde, G. R. (1998). *Formación Profesional y Sindicalismo en México*. Cinterfor. https://www.oitcinterfor.org/sites/default/files/file_articulo/wilde.pdf.

Epilogue

The presentation and analysis of the knowledge society and the education in Asia-Pacific: Recent trends and future challenges, shows the importance of science and technology for the development of all the countries, but particularly for those located in the Pacific Circle with a protagonist role in scientific progress. This is not only a consensus in the scientific literature but the indisputable global reality of the technological development of the twenty-first century.

Probably the examples that are present in this book are not enough to reach definitive conclusions about the knowledge society development in the Pacific Rim. However, these represent the scientific contributions of a group of researchers, members of the Pacific Circle Consortium whose interest in the subject contributes to explore this field of study with application in the classroom; considering the possibility for other countries to be included in a later book.

Given the current emergency caused by COVID-19, the world has confirmed the importance of science and technology in education. Firstly, because of the need to find a solution to the pandemic from the laboratory of the scientists committed to achieving a safer world. Secondly, by the extended use of ICT in a teaching process that is also transformed including topics such as sustainable development, artificial intelligence, civic engagement, and environmental. The former tendencies are testifying the continuous consolidation of the knowledge society.

Science has explored the importance of the knowledge society since several years, but the emergency of COVID-19 confirmed the importance for the inhabitants of the world to have the proper information and to avoid wrong decisions and actions.

COVID-19 has accelerated and broadened the Fourth Industrial Revolution with the rapid expansion of e-commerce, online education, digital health, and remote work. These shifts will continue to dramatically transform human interactions and livelihoods long after the pandemic is behind us. This change can provide huge benefits to societies—the response to COVID-19 is full of examples, from the ability to telework to the rapid development of a vaccine. However, these developments also risk exacerbating and creating inequalities. Respondents to the Global Risks

© The Editor(s) (if applicable) and The Author(s), under exclusive license to Springer Nature Singapore Pte Ltd. 2021
J. E. Rangel Delgado and A. Ivanova Boncheva (eds.), *Knowledge Society and Education in the Asia-Pacific*, SpringerBriefs in Education, https://doi.org/10.1007/978-981-16-2333-2

Perception Survey (GRPS) rated "digital inequality" both as a critical threat to the world over the next two years and the seventh most likely long-term risk.

In the context of this book, it is recognized that the population is increasingly informed because of the development of the internet, whose mismanagement can lead to the absence of values, hence the importance of an intelligent concatenation between science, technology, and education, which represents perhaps the greatest challenge of the knowledge society.

The contributions of this book about the practices of science, technology, and education, and the equitable access for all the people, illustrate the priority to focus on an inclusive and sustainable win-win formula with benefits for the great majority of the global society.

José Ernesto Rangel Delgado
Antonina Ivanova Boncheva